est entièrement inconnu

R. de Moscou qui tombe dans la baie de D...

Lac des Abitibi
Détroit de St Germain

Fort des Abitibie
Lac du Laborinte

Lac Temiscaming

PAYS DES

Ance à la Mine

Lac Caouinagame

Lau...

TEMIS CAMINGS

PAYS DES

I. Temiscaming   La Galete
I. Metabetchouan

NIPISSINGS

Long Sault
Rapide du Grenadier

Lac Nipissing

R. Acouinagouzin

Mataouan

Rivière

Portage de la Marquise
Portage Talon
Portage des Roses

Portage de l'Epine

Portage de Galete
Roch. capitaine
Port des
Toichons

R. Coeuse
Petite alumettes
du Borgne Les
Calumets

Portage

Coste n'est point connu

R. de Montaignes

R. des Sauteux

R. des Francois
ou il y a des Saults

ANCIEN PAYS

Grandes Alumettes
Portage de la Roche Fondut

R. de la Bonne chere

Outaouais

DES OUTAOUAIS

Lac Taronto

Lac Quentio

Lac S. Lion

NORD

I. de Cedanoyeux

Cannecouté

S. Marie
des Hurons
Petit lac des Hurons

Portage

Tannaout ové

Frontenac
aux Romain

R. de la Presqu I. I Bou't

R. St Laurent

Ici étoient
répandues

LES

IROQUOIS DU

Ganaraske

Kenté

Catadat Siagon

I aux Cerfs
I. du Large

B. de
Niaoure

HURON

ANCIEN
plusieurs Bourgades
PAYS DES de Hurons

Tejajagon

I aux Chevreuils
I aux Romain
I aux Galets

Nation du Petun
Détruite

Fond du Lac

LAC ONTARIO

P. de la Traverse

R. de l'Assomption

R. des Sables

HURONS

Ru qui a remonté ce dorate
ce jour braver de Sault

R. d'Uxeem la Grande Rivere

Quinaouatons

Sault de Niagara
de 250 pieds
au plus

des Sononontouans
Sonontouani
R. des Sables

R. St Plan

I. Ronde

R. Casconchiagon

Village de Missisaugues

Nation

R. d. Olier

Fort le grand Marais

F. de Chaumont
Lyene

F.
R. de
Chaumont

Lac de St Claire

Neutre Détruite

Le Petit
Lac

Riviere
inconnue

PAYS

F. des Sables

I. Tuscan

Techinoosen

Village d'Outaouais
R. des Cedres
Peau Etang
les Petits
Ecores

la Pointe aux Pins

la Pointe mouillee

Teennontouans

Fontaine brulante

Onontluaco

DES

Onnoutague
Onnontouan
Onnontouan

Aeniers
R. de la
Riviere

Detroit
la Pointe Pelee
Grands écores
la Longue Pointe

IROQUOIS

Aioc
Cayouder

Onnesteust

Lac Techirogen

LAC ERIÉ

Portage et Lac de
Karawangon

Ru Casconchiagon descend cette
Ru et remple de Sault ou Cascades

R. de Kanawango

L'egou de la Belle Riv...

Toute cette coste n'est presque point connue

Ce Canton etoit habité par les Erie
ou Nation du Chat qui a été detruite
par les Iroquois

R. Chaganon qui tombe dans la belle Riviere la belle

Portage

82 81 80 79 78 77

84 83 82 81 80 79 78 77

Yesterday's Michigan

FRANK ANGELO

Yesterday's
MICHIGAN

Seemann's Historic States Series No. 5

E. A. Seemann Publishing, Inc.
Miami, Florida

MW 6B RG

Many individuals and institutions kindly supported the author's task in collecting photographs. Their contributions are gratefully acknowledged (in abbreviated form) at the end of each caption:

AAA	*Motor News,* Automobile Club of Michigan	HPL	Hamtramck Public Library
Albion	Albion Historical Society	Interlochen	Interlochen Center for the Arts
Bay View	Bay View Association	Journal	*The Flint Journal*
Boyne	Boyne Mountain Lodge	Kimball	Kimball House Museum, Battle Creek
Bridge	Mackinac Bridge Authority		
Burton	Burton Historical Collection, Detroit Public Library	Kushner	Aid Kushner, Detroit
		Marshall	Marshall Historical Society Collection
Citizen	*Jackson Citizen Patriot*	MSU	Michigan State University
Clements	William L. Clements Library, University of Michigan	Muskegon	Muskegon Historical Museum
		MVMA	Motor Vehicle Manufacturers Association
Consumers	Consumers Power and Light, Jackson	News	*The Detroit News*
DFM	Detroit Federation of Musicians	Ohio	Ohio Historical Society Library
DHM	Detroit Historical Museum	Osgood	Dick Osgood, Farmington Hills
Dowling	Rev. Edward J. Dowling, Archivist, University of Detroit	Penobscot	City National Bank Building office
Enquirer	*Battle Creek Enquirer and News*	Petoskey	Petoskey Historical Society
Ferris	Ferris State College	Skillman	William M. Skillman, Detroit
Ford	Ford Archives	Smith	Gregory Smith, Boyne City
Forsythe	Robert Forsythe, Standish	State	Michigan Department of State Archives
Frankenmuth	Frankenmuth Historical Society		
Free Press	*The Detroit Free Press*	UCS	United Community Services, Detroit
Gale	Gale Research Company, Detroit		
Gazette	*The Kalamazoo Gazette*	U. of D.	University of Detroit Archives
General	General Telephone Company	U. of M.	University of Michigan News Department
GM	General Motors Corporation		
Grand	Grand Hotel, Mackinac Island	Vernor	Vernor's Ginger Ale, Detroit
Grand Rapids	Grand Rapids Public Library Archives	Wayne	Archives of Labor History, Wayne State University
Greenfield	Ford Museum, Greenfield Village	Willard	Willard Library, Battle Creek
Hinkle	Mary H. Hinkle, Venice, Fla.		
Houghton	Houghton County Historical Museum		

Library of Congress Cataloging in Publication Data

Angelo, Frank.
    Yesterday's Michigan.

    (Seemann's historic States series ; no. 5)
    Includes index.
    SUMMARY: Text and approximately 400 historical
photographs trace the history of Michigan from the
earliest settlement to the 1950's.
    1. Michigan--History--Pictorial works.
[1. Michigan--History--Pictorial works] I. Title.
F567.A53   977.4   75-45219
ISBN 0-912458-62-3

For Betty
Who Knows the Meaning
of Understanding

Contents

N O V V E L L E F R A N C
La Nation des Puans
Lac des Bisserenis
Sault
Petitte nation des Algommequins
Chasse des caribous
Algommequins
Grand lac
Mer douce
Descouuertures de ce grand lac, et de toutes ses terres depuis le sault St. Louis par le s. de Champlain, es années 1614. et 1615. iusques en l'an 1618
Hurons
Lac St Louis
Lac de Champlain
La nation neutre
Antouorons
Carantouanais
Virginia
Isle de l'Ascension
Baye de nostre Dame
C. Charles
C. Henry
Carte de la nouuelle france, augmentee depuis la derniere, seruant a la nauigation faicte en son vray Meridien, par le sr de Champlain Capitaine pour le Roy en la Marine, lequel depuis l'an 1603 iusques en l'annee 1629, a descouuert plusieurs costes, terres, lacs, riuieres, et Nations de sauuages, par cy deuant incognues, comme il se voit en ses relations qu'il a faict Imprimer en 1632. ou il se uoit cette marque ce sont habitations qu'ont faict les francois

ONE OF THE BOLDEST and most energetic of the early settlers was Samuel de Champlain, a navigator and cartographer, who put together this map in 1632 of what he saw and learned of the country himself and from others. A strong proponent of colonization, he "discerned in the magnificient prospect of the country which he occupied, the elements of a mighty empire." Note that there is no hint that Michigan would emerge as two peninsulas. (State)

Preface

THERE IS SOMETHING wonderful—and chastening—about taking on the task of putting together a history of a state that is so big in space and spirit as Michigan.

It's wonderful, of course, because it permits you to tell the story of what has been home for so many years with a sensitivity and feeling that is very personal, very private.

But then one is chastened by the magnitude of the task. For how do you really pull together all of the skeins of the tapestry of land and people and events, of tragedy and joy, and of victories and defeats, that have gone into building a home for nine million people today?

This, then, must go down simply as a gallant try, one that is unique in the way words and pictures are used.

You'll find few photos of things in this book. Instead, there's a procession of pictures of people, most showing them involved in activities—working, playing, crying, smiling, creative, and destructive. For that, in the end, is one of the least understood strengths about Michigan—the variety of people who poured into the state since the early 1800s. And this is true wherever one goes. A few trips, even today, confirm this fact. With my wife, Betty, I moved through the state in the summer of 1975, in order to prepare to write this history. We got as far north as Houghton on a day when the temperature hit 92, and we made more than a score of stops at other points east, west, and south.

Along the way, people, too many to name, gave of their time and offered their assistance to put into perspective the story of their town or their area or their region.

Two things stood out from these travels on a mission of history.

First, it is obvious that the scars that were left as our forebears swooped through the forests and the rivers are definitely being obliterated by the new growth of forests that rise skyward everywhere.

And second was the endless warmth of the people and their growing interest and awareness of our heritage. Everywhere, it seemed, an effort was being made to preserve and reconstruct the local story of the past—often with museums and displays of great imagination and value. Through these sources have come many of the pictures in this book, as noted on another page, and through them, too, has come great inspiration.

[9]

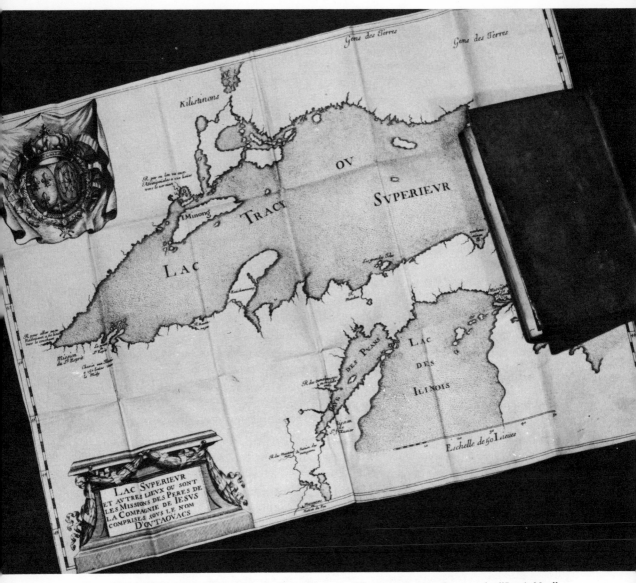

THE MOST ACCURATE MAP in the first 150 years of European exploration was the "Jesuit Map" published in 1670-71 in a book by Fr. Claude Dablon, who was superior of the Jesuit mission in Sault Ste. Marie. Of the map, he said. "It was got up by two fathers (presumably Allouez and Marquette), very intelligent and observing, who did not wish to incorporate anything except what they had seen with their own eyes." (Greenfield)

Two Peninsulas Emerge

IT TOOK several millions of years for nature to put together the lands, the trees, the minerals, and the waters that make up the State of Michigan.

The beginnings, when a nature that was brutal and beneficent by turns, gouged out the lakes, and spread a layer of good earth across what are now Michigan's two peninsulas, have gradually been pieced together by geologists and other scientists, but little is known yet of the very first Indians who came to make it home.

We need go back no further, however, than the early 1800s to find a point at which, suddenly, thousands of new people discovered the wonders of this wilderness and made it theirs.

Until that time, the land had been left almost entirely to the Indians, the *coureurs de bois*, the *voyageurs*, and a handful of mostly French clerics and adventurers who were impressed by its beauty and its potential for providing the good life. The first of the white men had seen the land in the early 1600s, but it wasn't until Antoine de la Mothe Cadillac established a post at Detroit in 1701 that people began to think of permanence, and it took more than a hundred years to convert that thought to reality.

In the meantime, men of many nations fought and died in their efforts to establish a foothold, until finally Michigan was part of the United States, and more people came and formed a government, and lived off the land and their skills, and built a community that became a leader in the quest for freedom—the freedom to move freely, and the freedom to live in dignity.

It was only about 10,000 years ago that the last of the glaciers left Michigan, and that the lakes and the trees and the fish and other forms of animal life began to flourish.

The Great Lakes, five of them—Superior, Huron, Michigan, Erie and Ontario—are unique. With their thousands of miles of shoreline, 6 trillion gallons of water, and their area of 95,170 square miles, they form the largest body of fresh water in the world. And Lake Superior is the largest single body of fresh water, ranging to a depth of 1,333 feet. Longfellow referred to it by the Indian name "Gitche Gumee," meaning "the shining Big Sea Water." The French called it *supérieur* for "upper lake," and others have called it many things to describe its periods of calm and roaring storms.

Through the lakes and the St. Lawrence River runs an unequalled inland waterway of 2,342 miles, starting from Duluth, Minnesota, to the open sea of the Atlantic, and two systems of locks help to lift and drop ships from Superior more than 600 feet above sea level to Ontario, only 245 feet above.

In addition, scattered through Michigan's 57,980 square miles of land, are 11,000 other lakes, the largest of which, Houghton, is 30.8 square miles, and many rivers, the longest of which is the 225-mile Grand. This Water Wonderland has shaped the way and quality of life of everyone from the first Indians who may have come 6,000 years ago to the millions of other people who followed.

The beauty of the area led men to speak of it in lyrical terms, and eventually the State made it official by adopting the motto, "If you seek a pleasant peninsula, look about you."

Before the white man came, Indians of many tribes roamed through the dense forests that covered most of the state, and some lived in buildings which were as much as sixty feet long and twelve feet wide and were used by several families, but they did not stay in one place long, and the land they tilled was in small parcels.

Samuel de Champlain, writing of their corn culture, is quoted as saying:

"They cleaned the land with great pains, though they had no proper instruments to do this. They trimmed all of the limbs from the trees which they burned at the foot of the trees which caused them to die. Then they thoroughly prepared the ground between the trees and planted their grain from step to step, putting in each hill about 10 grains and so continued until they had enough for three or four years' provision, lest a bad year, sterile and fruitless, befell them."

Michigan's Indian population, which is estimated at about 15,000 in the 1600s, belonged primarily to a common language group—the Algonguin, and the leading tribes were the Miami, Potawatomi, Sauk, Mascoutin, Chippewa or Ojibway, Ottawa, and Menominee. Generally speaking, the Chippewa or Ojibway lived in the Upper Peninsula, the Potawatomi in the valleys of the Kalamazoo, Huron, St. Joseph, and Raisin rivers, and the Sauk in the Saginaw Valley.

While the Indians' culture changed rapidly with the coming of the white man, particularly because of their exposure to liquor, they made significant contributions to the building of the state. In the early days, they served as guides. They trapped the animals which provided the furs that for two centuries were basic to commercial growth. They taught the white man how to raise corn, and introduced him to tobacco and how to make the birch bark canoe. And it was the Indian who blazed the trails through the wilderness that the white man eventually would follow in building his railroads and highways.

Champlain was the first among the French to envision the greatness of the North American interior. Having already helped to colonize Nova Scotia, which the French called Acadia, Champlain pushed into the St. Lawrence River and founded Quebec City on July 3, 1608.

He befriended the Hurons and helped them to fight the Iroquois—an act which would profoundly affect the direction and pace of development of America's interior, including

WHAT STARTED as a quest for a route to the East turned into development of an entirely new business for France—the fur trade. First men adopted the peltry for ornamentation and wear, but use spread even beyond France, and furs became a sign of social status and of office, such as the ermine robes for judges. All of which helped to make even greater the drive for fur-trade profits.

Michigan. Champlain's action earned him and the French the long-lasting enmity of the Iroquois who controlled lakes Ontario and Erie, and the French were forced to explore by more difficult routes, when they could explore at all.

In 1615, Champlain journeyed up the Ottawa River, crossed the portage at Lake Nipissing, and reached Georgian Bay. While he himself did not go to Michigan, he trained many men, and two of them, Etienne Brulé in 1618 and Jean Nicolet in 1634, are credited with being the first white men to see Michigan's Upper Peninsula.

Thus did Champlain plant the seed for establishing a New France.

It flourished in the early years because Richelieu and Louis XIV encouraged colonization, but European wars that created problems in the homeland, personal intrigues and the strength of the Iroquois, who were aided and abetted by the Dutch and the English, combined to stymie the French development.

Besides exploration and the fur trade, the French zealously pursued missionary work, particularly among their friends, the Hurons. Jesuit fathers Isaac Jogues and Charles Raymbault, who had been working with the Hurons in an area they called Huronia near Georgian Bay, reached the St. Mary's River in 1641. But thereafter the Iroquois effectively stopped major exploration efforts until the late 1660s.

As they moved northward in Canada, the Iroquois virtually eliminated the Hurons and cut off even the northern passage of exploration. Finally, in desperation, Louis XIV sent a force of more than 1,200 men to attack the Iroquois in 1664, and in 1667 they agreed to a treaty which lasted about twenty years.

DRESSED IN DAMASK presumably to impress the people of China whom he had hoped to find, Jean Nicolet landed in the Upper Peninsula in 1634. A protege of Samuel de Champlain, Nicolet is generally considered to be the first white man who most assuredly set foot on Michigan soil. Etienne Brule, who traveled into the area in 1618, also may have landed here. This mural was part of Michigan's exhibit at 1933 Chicago World Fair. (State)

FOR THE FIRST TIME, at the bottom of this map drawn in 1681, the name "Michigami" appears. (Greenfield)

[14]

Developments came relatively fast in this period of tenuous peace.

First came Fr. Jacques Marquette who was described as of "gentle, joyous disposition, ever looking upon the bright side of life, burning with that zeal which has through all time inspired the martyrs of religious faith." He established a mission at Sault Ste. Marie in 1668, and another one at St. Ignace three years later.

Continuing the search for that elusive waterway to the East, Fr. Marquette joined Louis Joliet in 1673 to explore for the Mississippi River of which the Indians spoke. They went by way of the Wisconsin River, then got as far as the mouth of the Arkansas River.

Meanwhile Adrien Joliet, older brother of Louis, investigated the possibility of mining copper, and became the first white man known to land in the Lower Peninsula when he headed for Montreal in 1669. An Iroquois guide took him along the east coast, through Lake St. Clair, the Detroit River and to Lake Erie. He proceeded overland from there.

It was during this time also that Louis XIV, having established New France as a royal colony in 1663, moved to strengthen his claim to the interior of North America by having Simon François, sieur de St. Lusson, stage a pageant at the Sault. A conclave of natives was brought together in 1671 to witness a ceremony during which "all the lands bounded on the one end by the Northern and Western seas and on the other by the South Sea, including its length and breadth" were claimed for the king.

To give tangible support to those claims, there appeared Robert Cavalier de la Salle who was determined to set up a line of forts from Lake Ontario to the Gulf of Mexico to thwart any challenges by Spain or England. He built the first one at Fort Niagara, and during 1679 he also built the *Griffon*, the first sailing vessel to navigate the Great Lakes.

LaSalle sailed the *Griffon* to Mackinac and then to Green Bay, where it was loaded with furs and headed back to Niagara on September 18. LaSalle stayed behind to pursue his explorations—and never saw the *Griffon* again. To this day, its fate remains buried on a lake bottom.

LaSalle left Mackinac with four canoes and 14 men after the *Griffon's* departure and established a fort at the mouth of the St. Joseph River on November 1, 1679, then set out to reach the Mississippi. That effort was cut short, however, when he was convinced that the *Griffon* was missing. On March 20, 1680, he set out on foot across the southern part of Michigan and became, as far as is known, the first white man to move across the interior of the Lower Peninsula. LaSalle did come back later and reached the mouth of the Mississippi in 1682.

[15]

INDIANS WHO LIVED in Michigan as much as 6,000 years ago left behind many artifacts, such as this collection of spears and arrowheads. Many signs of their mining for copper have been found in the Upper Peninsula and on Isle Royale, and things made of Michigan's uniquely pure brand of copper also have been found in many other areas of the country. (State)

AS THE FUR TRADE GREW, a breed of men came on the scene who made it their way of life. The *coureurs de bois* were unlicensed traders who are described as having a "strange mixture of civilization and savage." Aiding them and other traders were the *voyageurs* who paddled the canoes that carried the furs and supplies. One hundred miles was considered by some as a day's journey, and "fifty songs a day were as nothing" to them, according to one typically exuberant *voyageur*. Competition was keen as suggested by this sketch of traders racing for the shore which appeared in *Harpers Magazine*.

[16]

VOYAGEURS in camp for the night as depicted in a *Harpers* sketch.

While priests and adventurers worked valiantly to seek new souls and new lands, a great battle was going on for control of the fur trade which had sparked much of the exploration in the first place. Those who had monopoly charters for the business wanted trading concentrated in Montreal, but horizons had been broadened and the *coureurs de bois*, bartering with the natives directly, paid little attention to such niceties as charters.

However, the monopolists did have, indirectly, the support of the Jesuits who were incensed by the use traders made of liquor in their dealings with the Indians. The Jesuits felt the flow of liquor also could be controlled by centering trade in one area. Eventually, they convinced Louis XIV of the wisdom of such a plan, and in 1696 he ordered abandonment of all western posts, except one at St. Louis.

It is at this point that Cadillac, an implacable foe of the Jesuits, took center stage in the history of Michigan.

As indicated, the French were first confined to the upper country because of the threats of the Iroquois, but as the French opened up the territory, the Iroquois and the British tried to win over the Indians in the area. So the French decided to put up additional forts. One at what is now Port Huron was held only briefly, but they materially strengthened their hold to the north.

In 1690, Louis de Buade, Comte de Frontenac, considered one of the greatest of all governors of New France, decided to locate a garrisoned fort at St. Ignace where about 7,000 Huron and Ottawa Indians lived near the mission. He called it Fort de Buade and picked Cadillac as its commandant in 1694.

The King's order to shut down forts upset Cadillac. He went to Europe in 1699 and convinced Count Pontchartrain, the chief minister, to send him to Detroit as part of a new start toward French domination of the West.

Cadillac proposed that this new post be a colony, and that he would take with him farmers and artisans. He would be a *seigneur* with rights to grant land and to receive tolls for rendering services, such as grinding grain.

Cadillac also suggested that he would invite Indians to come and live near this colony to learn French customs and culture, and, of course, to trade their furs at his post. In fact, groups of Ottawas, Chippewas, Hurons, and Miamis did come to live in the vicinity of Detroit and, it is said, they called Cadillac "our father."

Cadillac used the Ottawa River-Lake Nipissing-Georgian Bay route, reached the Detroit river on July 23, 1701, and landed on the American side the next day because a high bluff and the Savoyard River would make it easier to defend against possible attacks.

Cadillac was at Detroit for nine years, and was a strong and controversial leader. Ironically, the invitation he extended to the Fox Indians of Wisconsin was belatedly accepted and caused Detroit's only major problem for the next forty years. Arrival of the Fox stirred the animosity of other tribes, and a brief war ensued during which the Fox laid siege to Detroit for several days.

After their departure and pursuit by other Indians who annihilated the group, calm settled in Michigan.

In his history, Prof. Willis F. Dunbar says of the period:

[17]

AMONG THE MORE FAMOUS of the early contributors to Michigan history is Fr. Jacques Marquette who established the first mission at Sault Ste. Marie in 1668. This sketch shows Marquette getting a geography lesson from Indians and was made by Father Jacker in St. Ignace, where Marquette also ran a mission.

THE MOST NOTABLE of the seventeenth century explorers as far as Michigan is concerned was probably Robert Cavalier, sieur de la Salle, who is rated "a man of genius, enterprise and undoubted talent." Desiring to expand the French empire, he built the first sailing ship to travel on the Great Lakes, started a series of fortifications, and became the first white man to penetrate the interior of the Lower Peninsula. Eventually, he was successful in reaching the mouth of the Mississippi and laying claim to Louisiana for the French. (State)

"The fertile soil yielded good crops without much labor and there were no markets for surplus products; hence the habitants took life easy. They raised large families, and their sons and daughters married at an early age. They were devoted to their church, but they also were a merry lot with their songs and cart racing. . . . There were only occasional travelers to bring news of the outside world. All in all it was an isolated and, in a sense, idyllic life that Detroiters lived in this period."

Resolution of the duel for empire between the French and English brought the next major change in Michigan's development.

Three days after the French surrender of Canada to the British in September 1760, Maj. Robert Rogers was assigned to take over the French posts in Michigan. He arrived with 200 men in Detroit on November 29.

Insight into the state of development of Michigan at this point comes from the words of two eye witnesses.

On December 2, Capt. John Campbell, who had accompanied Rogers to Detroit and became the first British commandant, wrote:

"The inhabitants seem very happy at the change of government but they are in great want of everything. The fort is much better than we expected. It is one of the best stockades I have ever seen, but the Commandant's house and what belongs to the King is in bad repair."

And Alexander Henry, writing in his "Travels" book, had this to say about Michilimackinac:

"Within the stockade are 30 houses, neat in their appearance and tolerably commodious, and a church in which Mass is celebrated by a Jesuit missionary. The number of

IT WAS 1701 and Michigan got its first permanent settlement, on the shores of the Detroit River. Antoine de la Mothe Cadillac landed and built Fort Pontchartrain, named for the French minister who had commissioned him and provided a grant of 15 acres "wherever on the Detroit the new fort should be established." Cadillac was soon joined by his wife Therese and by habitants, who established the famed strip farms along both sides of the river. Cadillac himself, who had earned the enmity of the Jesuits because of his resistance to their plan to ban liquor to the Indians, was eventually assigned to be governor of Louisiana in 1710.

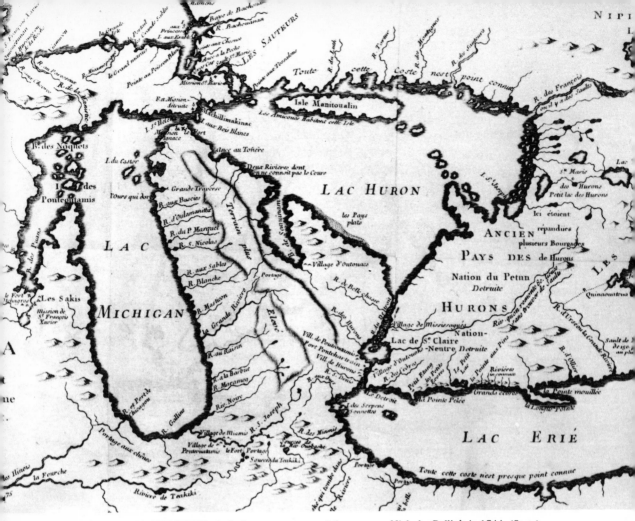

ONE OF THE FIRST relatively accurate maps of the area was Nicholas Bellin's in 1744. (State)

families may be nearly equal to that of the houses, and their subsistence is derived from the Indian traders, who assemble here in their voyages to and from Montreal. Michilimackinac is the place of deposit and point of departure between the upper country and the lower."

Small detachments took over the forts at Sault Ste. Marie and the post on the St. Joseph river. Thus ended the French phase of Michigan history.

Hardly had the British settled in, however, when they faced a challenge from the Indians. Their relations differed sharply from those which the French had established.

Jeffrey Amherst, the British commander of Canada, was opposed to what he considered coddling of the natives, and he banned liquor and the giving of presents to them. The British also closed the area west of the Alleghenies to settlement from the colonies.

Thus, their policies antagonized both the Indians and the colonists, who continued to find their way across the mountains anyway.

Independent traders, as usual, paid little attention to the regulations, but they contributed to Indian resentment by giving them bad liquor, shoddy goods at high prices, and by forcing them to come to the forts to sell their furs.

Against this backdrop a great Indian uprising occurred in 1763 which finally centered around Detroit because it was the only fort west of Pittsburgh to survive the widespread Indian assaults triggered by the Senecas in New York.

A leading character in the drama was Pontiac, an Ottawa chieftain, who lived near Detroit. By all accounts, he was smart, smooth, and articulate, and he convinced the Chippewas, Hurons, and Potawatomi living nearby to attack Detroit.

Pontiac's plan involved leading a group, carrying guns under their blankets, into the fort for a conference with the British commandant, Henry Gladwin. At a signal, the guns were to be turned on Gladwin and others. Gladwin learned of the plot, however, and when Pontiac reached for the wampum that served as a signal, Gladwin's officers drew their swords and drums rolled in the barracks. It was then that Gladwin stepped up to one of the Indians, pulled aside his blanket to reveal the shortened guns.

In the days that followed, there was bloodshed, and it wasn't until 153 days later that a siege imposed by Pontiac ended. Eventually, on July 23, 1766, Pontiac signed a treaty of peace proclaiming his allegiance to the British.

When Rogers took over Detroit, it was a town of 300 houses and 2,000 inhabitants. The French *habitants* were scattered along the river on both sides for several miles and were totally indifferent to the government, since most of them did not even live within the fortified area.

Things had changed very little by the time of Independence in 1776. There were Indians, British soldiers, and the French in Michigan, all of them quite comfortable with the British side. The land was still wild. Only the fur trader and soldier in the forts symbolized the King of England's rule.

[21]

HOW DETROIT SHAPED UP in 1760 when the British took over is depicted in this map which may have been drawn by William Brazier, a draughtsman and surveyor for the British at that time. The small inset showing the western approach to the fort is described as the first contemporary view of Detroit. The original map was recently obtained by the Detroit Public Library's Burton Collection.

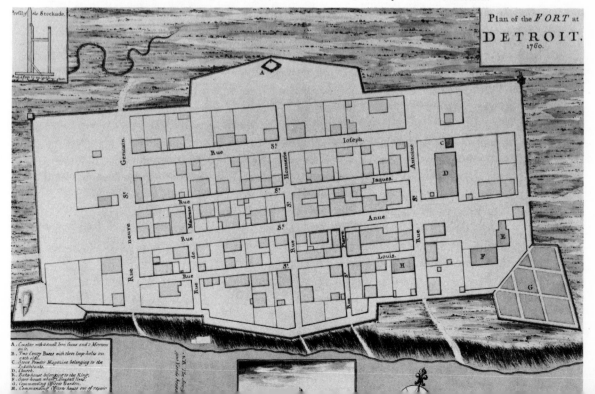

A GREAT UPRISING by the Indians in 1763 threatened the British hold on the West, and great cunning was used by them in some instances. For example, the Ojibway and Sacs appeared at Fort Michilimackinac, the only other major site in Michigan besides Detroit, on June 4, the birthday of King George. Presumably, they would entertain the garrison outside of the fort with a game of baggataway, played with a ball batted about in the style of lacrosse today. But by design, at one point the ball was hit into the fort and the players headed for its gate, snatching hatchets which spectator squaws had hid under their blankets. Amid whoops, the players-turned-warriors fell on the garrison, slaughtering everyone except a few men who managed to slip away.

Although few of the white settlers who crossed the mountains from the colonies were here, the area inevitably was involved in the Revolution because Massachusetts, Connecticut, and Virginia each had charter claims to all or part of what is now Michigan. Their charters had provided for control of land from sea-to-sea at a time when no one really had known what that encompassed.

In other areas of the West, however, there had been extensive settlement. Instead of making friends with these people, who might have been won over because they felt left out by the colonists, the British turned loose Indians to scalp and attack, and they lost the possibility of their support.

It brought a counter attack, instead, led by George Rogers Clark, who was placed in command of Virginia troops in 1778 and captured Kaskaskia in the Illinois Territory on July 4. He also took Cahokia and then Vincennes under extraordinary circumstances.

Henry Hamilton, British commander at Detroit, attacked and won Vincennes in December 1778, and Clark decided quickly to risk everything on a single battle, because he did not want the British to solidify their control.

In February 1779, Clark set out from Kaskaskia with 130 men during an unusually rainy period, and they marched through water which at times was two to four feet deep. Quite bedraggled, hungry, tired, and cold, they finally reached Vincennes, made a show of strength, and after a series of talks forced Hamilton's unconditional surrender on March 5.

That secured the Ohio Valley and, many feel, the West for the United States in one of the most daring feats in American history.

IT WAS NOT UNTIL 1796 that Detroit finally and firmly became part of the United States, and a campaign by Gen. "Mad Anthony" Wayne was decisive. While the Revolution ended in the East, there was much fighting among Indians and white settlers in the West. In a victorious battle at Fallen Timbers (an area where trees had been uprooted by a tornado) and a peace conclave at Greenville *(above)*, Wayne succeeded in solving the problem. (Ohio)

AFTER MUCH RESEARCH, the Detroit Historical Society was able to find this authentic portrait of Gen. Anthony Wayne which was painted by Jean Pierre Henri Elouis in Philadelphia during the early part of 1796. General Wayne, who was in Detroit in August of that year, became ill and died in Erie, Pennsylvania, en route home. (DHM)

There was one other incident of note affecting Michigan before the Revolutionary War ended. In 1781, the Spanish attacked Fort Miami on the St. Joseph and held it for a short time. Since the fort was located near the site of the present city of Niles, that community has the distinction of being the only one in Michigan which has been under four flags, French, British, Spanish, and American.

There followed a period when, despite the end of the war, Michigan's relationship to the United States was rather tenuous.

Benjamin Franklin was one of the three commissioners who dealt for peace with England and had a hand in keeping the West for the States by a compromise that allowed Britain to keep Canada.

During these negotiations, however, the British refused to give up their hold on Michigan, so the area was included in a civil government which the British set up for what was called Upper Canada. An election was held in 1792, and the Detroit area, with the bulk of the population, was entitled to three representatives in the elective assembly which met in Niagara on September 12. Finally, by the Jay Treaty in 1794, jurisdiction over the Northwest Territory which Congress had established in 1784 was extended over the lands given up by the British.

One other problem persisted, however. It centered on trying to settle the question of Indian claims and settlers' claims, and it led to one attack after another. In one instance an American army detachment was routed in an Indian attack, and 620 men were killed, 283 wounded.

"Mad Anthony" Wayne was called on, and he organized an army of about 2,500 men and advanced from Cincinnati on October 18, 1793. He won a decisive battle against the Indians at Fallen Timbers, then returned to Greenville where early in 1795 a treaty was signed and a modicum of peace was achieved.

[24]

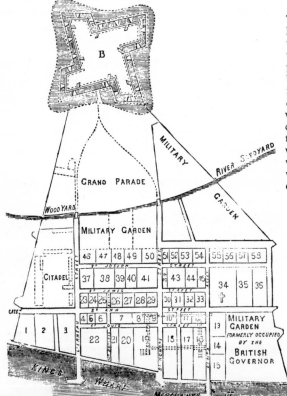

THE AMERICAN FLAG went up in Detroit on July 11, 1796, and at the time Fort Lernoult (indicated by B at top of drawing) was located above the palisaded village itself. It had been built by the British in the 1780s. This map is included in E. L. Sheldon's *Early History of Michigan,* printed in 1856, and so were comments by the Rev. O. M. Spencer, who provided an excellent description of the city when he said: "Detroit was then a small town, containing only wooden buildings, but few of which were well finished, surrounded by high pickets enclosing an area of probably half a mile square, about one-third of which, along the bank of the river, as the Strait was called, was covered with houses. There were, I think, four narrow streets running parallel to the river and intersected by four or five more at right angles."
(DHM-Gale)

More than a thousand persons from many tribes attended. They feasted and were entertained. Present were Little Turtle, Blue Jacket, Red Pole, Little Beaver, and Little Horn, and the treaty which was concluded provided for a definite line between native and white lands.

In return for $20,000 worth of goods and a promise of an annual gift of $9,500 in supplies, the Indians conceded about two-thirds of the present state of Ohio. The Indians also gave up their claims to certain land in Michigan—a strip six miles wide along the Detroit River for a distance of more than forty miles—from the Raisin River to Lake St. Clair. The lands around Detroit and around Mackinac also were ceded.

A force under Col. John Francis Hamtramck later was sent to Detroit to occupy it on July 11, 1796. Wayne himself arrived on August 13. He stayed a few days, but on his way home, he was taken ill and died in Erie, Pennsylvania.

The Battle of Fallen Timbers, the Treaty of Greenville, and the coming of Hamtramck ended another era in the story of Michigan, and in a real sense wrote finis to the Revolutionary War.

What were conditions in Michigan at the moment?

Detroit and Mackinac were the major centers in the area, with a few white settlers on the Kalamazoo, St. Joseph, and Grand rivers in the western part, and a few more along the River Raisin and near the present city of Monroe.

In Detroit, there were about five-hundred inhabitants, most of French ancestry. They spoke French and observed the rites of the Catholic Church. Merchants and traders were chiefly English and Scotch. There were a few Americans already in town, a number of Indian slaves, and blacks, some free and some slaves. In spite of the Northwest Ordinance, those who had slaves when Americans took over were permitted to keep them.

John Askin, James May, William Macomb, and Joseph Campau were among the names of merchants in the Detroit area. St. Anne's Church ministered to the spiritual needs, and there was a Masonic lodge, Zion Lodge No. 10, which had been formed during the British period.

The fort, which the British had expanded in the 1780s and called Lernoult, was the center of town. Within it were the barracks and shops. Just below the fort, the town had about 100 houses, most of them built of logs, and the river was filled with sloops, schooners, and canoes.

A notable event in Michigan history occurred on January 18, 1802, when the territorial government approved incorporation of Detroit. It provided for a five-man board of trustees and an annual meeting for voters.

The trustees were authorized to take whatever action was deemed necessary for the health and welfare of the inhabitants, and their chief concern seems to have been the threat of fire. A code was quickly adopted which provided for regular chimney sweeping, ladders, buckets, and barrels, and it was everyone's duty to turn out to fight a fire.

The second ordinance they passed regulated trade. Bakers were required to sell a three-pound loaf for six pence and to stamp their initials on each loaf.

Income for the town government for the fiscal year 1803-04 was $137.25. After paying out the fees to officers and 15 dollars to repair the fire engine, the town had a surplus of $35.56.

Statehood talk was quick to develop, and the first step was taken on January 11, 1805, when the Congress passed an act setting up the Territory of Michigan. It became effective on June 30 of that year, when there were only four villages in its borders—Detroit, Sault Ste. Marie, Mackinac, and Monroe—and the state's population was about 5,000.

The name Michigan, formally adopted at that time, derived from the Algonquin word Michigamea, and means literally "a great lake."

Nine years had elapsed since the Americans came, but little had changed. Fr. Gabriel Richard had arrived in Detroit in June 1798, and the first Protestant missionary, the Rev. David Bacon, came in 1800. Detroit had five doctors of medicine and a number of private schools.

On June 11, 1805, just a few days before Michigan officially became a territory, a fire that was started by some ashes from the pipe of baker John Harvey, destroyed Detroit. After valiant efforts with axes, battering rams, and a bucket brigade to bring water directly from the river, all that was left standing was an old warehouse and several stone chimneys.

Father Richard was among those stunned by the catastrophe, but in a short time he had mustered the French farmers along the river to provide food, shelter, and solace.

In a way, it was an incredible coincidence that this fire should happen hours before Michigan's first territorial officials were to arrive.

William Hull of Massachusetts was chosen governor. He was a lawyer, a graduate of Yale, and a veteran of the Revolution. He was fifty-two years old, but he lacked experience with life on the frontier.

Stanley Griswold was appointed secretary, and one of the three judges selected was Augustus Elias Brevoort Woodward, a young man of thirty-one who was born in New York and had moved to Virginia at twenty-one. He became a good friend of Thomas Jefferson, who chose him for the Michigan post.

Faced with a catastrophe, Hull and Woodward went to Washington to get approval of a plan that would add 10,000 acres to the city and would provide each citizen over seventeen years of age with a lot of not less than 5,000 square feet, a good-sized lot even in today's market. Woodward also came out of Washington with a copy of Maj. Pierre l'Enfant's plan for that Capitol city, which he tried to adapt for Detroit.

In the years that followed, Hull, Woodward, and James Witherell of Vermont, who had succeeded John Frederick Bates of Detroit as another of the judges, moved to enact laws to provide for more civil control, and progress was gradually being made when suddenly Detroit faced another of its major crises—the War of 1812.

Congress declared war on June 18, but for some reason word did not reach Hull until July 1, and by that time a series of events had been put in motion which eventually led to

THE BLOODIEST BATTLE ever fought in Michigan occurred in 1813, when the American flag went up again—this time to stay—over the fort at Detroit. That was insured by the victory of Oliver Hazard Perry in the famed Battle of Lake Erie *(above)*. Before that, however, came resounding defeat. On the morning of January 22, 1813, a British force with strong support from the Indians completely surprised an American force of about one thousand at Frenchtown (now Monroe) on the River Raisin *(below)*. Only about sixty survivors found their way back to the Maumee River. It was the high point of British success in the West during the War of 1812. Meanwhile, Perry through the winter of 1812-1813 was building a fleet which in September met and defeated the British in Lake Erie.

THIS PORTRAIT OF OLIVER Hazard Perry helped to idealize his victory. (DHM)

the surrender of Detroit on August 15. Hull later was court-martialed for his action, convicted, and pardoned.

It was the decision to entrust a young lieutenant, Oliver Hazard Perry, with the task of building a fleet that finally turned the tide in the war. Perry built seven small schooners, three brigs, and two gunboats, and toward the end of July 1813, he received a complement of 70 men whom he characterized as "a motley set, blacks, soldiers, boys."

A hundred more came a few days later, and Perry's forces went out to meet the British on Lake Erie, making contact at about noon on September 10. By nightfall he had sent his famous message, "We have met the enemy and they are ours."

On September 30, Detroit was retaken, and thus was concluded still another Michigan chapter. With it came the end of the Indian menace to Detroit, a firm hold on the land by the United States, and a new expansion-conscious administration led by Lewis Cass.

Near an end, too, was the fur trade as a major factor, and at hand was the coming of the farmers and artisans out of the East to help create an unusual heritage for Michigan.

[28]

Then Came the Settlers

"I HAVE NO HESITATION to say that it would be to the advantage of the Government to remove every inhabitant of the Territory, pay for the improvements and reduce them to ashes, leaving nothing but the garrison posts. From my observation, the Territory appears to be not worth defending and merely a den for Indians and Traitors. The banks of the Detroit River are handsome but nine-tenths of the land in the Territory is unfit for cultivation."

In the face of such words, a new era was bound to begin, and begin it did. The words were written by Gen. Duncan MacArthur who was stationed in Detroit and who was replying to a letter written by William Woodbridge of Ohio.

Woodbridge had been appointed to join Gov. Lewis Cass as secretary of the territory, but before accepting he sought information about conditions.

Obviously, MacArthur's opinion could not have been lower. Yet, Woodbridge came to Michigan, and so did thousands of others within a few years.

The end of the War of 1812 found the state with a population of about four-thousand, with new administrative leadership, and with all its natural resources except for fur-bearing animals virtually untouched. Southern Michigan was covered with maple, oak, elm, hickory, ash, and birch. Unfortunately, a government survey report issued in Washington had expressed an opinion comparable to MacArthur's.

Signed by Edwin Tiffin, Surveyor General of the United States, the report was based on findings from the field that suggested that Michigan was pretty much all swamps, lakes, and sandy soil. Tiffin concluded that "not more than one acre in a hundred, if there were one out of a thousand that would in any case admit of cultivation."

Cass had to combat the impact of that statement and had to face the prospect of negotiating further treaties with the Indians to clear the way for the expansion he wanted. He succeeded in both instances. By the time Michigan was admitted to the Union, only the western part of the Upper Peninsula had not been ceded by Indian Treaty, and he took a 4,200-mile, four-month long trip in 1820 that carried him into all sections of the Territory and dramatized its viability.

FOR ALMOST TWO DECADES, Lewis Cass was the dominant figure in Michigan development. He was born in Exeter, New Hampshire; studied at Phillip Academy; and became a lawyer in Marietta, Ohio, before serving in the War of 1812. Cass became territorial governor in 1813, and served until 1831. He personally took the lead in arranging several treaties with the Indians, and did much to launch road building and other projects to help the state grow. (Gale)

INDIAN TITLE to lands in Michigan was gradually relinquished starting with the Treaty of Greenville in 1795, but a major cession came in 1819 when the Treaty of Saginaw was signed, with Gov. Lewis Cass playing a major role. Because settlers had shown an interest, the U.S. government instructed Cass to deal with the Indians in the Saginaw Valley. He arranged a large gathering on September 10, when the Indians had harvested their grain but had not started winter hunting. Jacob Smith, a man who had lived among the Indians, was given land to get him to help make the deal, and $3,000 silver dollars were piled on a table. Cass proposed to buy some six million acres with this, plus an annual payment of $10.000. Louis Campau, a former Detroiter and founder of Saginaw, claimed $1,500 of the money but was dissuaded from interfering by other traders. Finally, the treaty was signed, and Cass broke out five barrels of liquor to celebrate the occasion.

THE FIRST DELEGATE to Congress from the Michigan Territory was William Woodbridge, whose family had moved from Connecticut to Marietta, Ohio, when he was eleven. Woodbridge served as Indian agent, and then was named territorial secretary with Gov. Lewis Cass. He was elected to Congress in 1819, where he served one year. He later was a judge, and in 1839 he became the state's second elected governor. (DHM)

In the meantime, two other major events were developing that would help spark Michigan's growth because they would provide the mobility that made the difference.

In 1818, the *Walk-in-the-Water*, the first steamship on the Great Lakes, made its inaugural trip to Detroit from Buffalo, and at the same time plans were being completed for building of the Erie Canal from Albany on the Hudson to Buffalo, New York. Cass also succeeded in getting Congress to appropriate money for roads, several of which were built in the 1820s following the Indian trails that had been used for years.

Later, Fr. Gabriel Richard, who was elected to Congress in 1823, successfully sponsored a bill for construction of a road between Detroit and Chicago which took ten years to build, and was completed in 1835.

By 1832 most of the major roads that exist today had been started, and the railroads were to follow soon.

Gradually along the trails, for in truth the roads were no more than strips through the forests, the cities of the future began to grow. A group of Detroiters planned Pontiac in 1818 on the Saginaw Trail where it crossed the Clinton River, and farther along Flint emerged from a fur trading post built in 1819 by Jacob Smith at a ford in the Flint River.

Louis Campau, an independent fur trader from Detroit, platted the town of Saginaw in 1822, and later moved to the western part of Michigan to found Grand Rapids.

Ypsilanti, begun in 1824, was named for an heroic Greek leader, and John Allen and Elisha Walker Rumsey came upon a burr oak opening where a creek flowed into the Huron River, where they laid out a town and named it after their wives, both named Ann. Ann Arbor became the county seat in 1826, and by 1836 had a population of about 2,000.

Jackson in 1829, and Albion, Kalamazoo, Marshall, and Battle Creek, in 1831, joined the swelling list of Michigan towns.

Little wonder, therefore, that at this time the demand for full statehood became a primary concern—and with good reason.

Suddenly, Michigan's population, which was 8,765 in 1820, had surged to 87,278 by

ABOUT THE TIME William Woodbridge was being given scare stories about Michigan, this is one artist's view of how Detroit and its harbor appeared.

MINISTERING TO the spiritual needs of about 7,000 Catholics (as of 1826) was a primary task for Fr. Gabriel Richard, but he also played a major role in education and politics. He arrived in Detroit in 1798 to share responsibility for Saint Anne's parish, founded in 1701. He helped to establish schools in Detroit and tried to do the same in Monroe and Mackinac. In 1823, he was one of six candidates for Congress and was elected because of solid French support. He died in 1832 while caring for victims in Detroit's first major cholera epidemic. (Gale)

IT WASN'T UNTIL 1818 that the first Methodist Church was built, as early settlers had been primarily of the Catholic faith. This log cabin, located on the Rouge River, was the first Protestant house of worship in the territory.

[32]

1834, and was on its way to 212,267 in 1840, 397,654 in 1850, and 749,113 on the eve of the Civil War.

Playing a leading role in the drive was Stevens T. Mason, who had become territorial secretary in 1831 at age nineteen, and was acting governor in 1834 after the death of George B. Porter. Mason also became the first elected leader after Statehood.

A constitutional convention was held in 1835 which came up with a document particularly emphasizing education. One of its provisions was for appointment of a state superintendent of schools, the first such in any state in the Union. It also provided for payment of $3 a day to legislators, and that wasn't changed until 1948!

It wasn't until January 26, 1837, that Pres. Andrew Jackson signed the bill making Michigan the 26th state, and it came about only after a series of rather wild incidents which even included a threat of war between Michigan and Ohio. But this blew over, no one got hurt, and Michigan received the Upper Peninsula in exchange for a strip of land that included Toledo.

In 1818, the first government land office was opened in Detroit followed by others around the state, and by 1825, most of the southern one-third of the Lower Peninsula had been surveyed into one-mile square sections (640 acres) and six-mile square townships, and land sales were booming at $1.25 an acre. "Michigan fever" reached a peak when 4 million acres were sold in 1836.

Newcomers were mostly from the New England states, but by 1825 many Germans and Irish came in the first major foreign migration, with many of the Germans moving into the Ann Arbor and Saginaw Valley area to farm. By 1860, aside from the immigrants from the British Isles, the Germans were by far the largest ethnic group in Michigan with 38,787. The Dutch, most of them living in the western part of the state, totaled 6,335, and there were 6,794 blacks, 1,673 in Wayne County and 1,368 in Cass County.

Schools, newspapers, and churches had begun to flourish. In 1817, a state university which Judge Augustus Woodward called the Catholepistemaid for the University of Michigama was started in Detroit, and moved to Ann Arbor in 1841. In 1857, Michigan became the first state to establish an agricultural college, and Kalamazoo College became the first denominational school chartered by the state in 1833.

Michigan also was enjoying a boom—the final one—in the fur trading era. John Jacob Astor became the dominant factor, operating out of Mackinac Island. He reportedly cleared as much as one and two million dollars a year during the 17 years he was president of the American Fur Trading Company.

And there was the beginning of the exploitation of Michigan's lumber and mineral resources. A copper rush started in the early 1840s; iron ore was discovered about the same time; and the Soo locks were built in the 1850s to accommodate the great flow of material to the mills of the south.

Michigan, as always, was playing a major role in the political life of the nation which was deeply immersed in an intense debate over the slavery issue. Lewis Cass, who had resigned as territorial governor in 1831 to become Secretary of War in Pres. Andrew Jackson's cabinet, found himself at odds with his former constituency.

[34]

PEOPLE POURED into Michigan in the 1830s with the availability of transportation from the East, particularly the Erie Canal. The canal, completed in 1825, ran through the Mohawk Valley and included several locks. Despite the fact that horses were used to pull the barges, it cut travel time from the East by days. Coupled with the appearance in 1818 of the first steamship, the *Walk-in-the-Water* which made its maiden voyage from Buffalo to Detroit, the canal made possible a whole new approach to the West for thousands.

TO EMIGRANTS AND TRAVELERS.

The Erie and Kalamazoo Railroad is now in full operation between

Toledo and Adrian.

During the ensuing season trains of cars will run daily to Adrian, there connecting with a line of stages for the West, Michigan City, Chicago and Wisconsin Territory.

Emigrants and others destined for Indiana, Illinois and Western Michigan,

WHILE SHIPS AND CANALS brought people in, roads and railroads were being built to provide additional mobility. In 1836, the Erie and Kalamazoo line reached Adrian from Toledo, never going any farther; but it was the first railroad line in the state. Although horses hauled the cars first, in 1837 a locomotive was obtained. The above was part of an advertisement promoting the road. There were those who traveled by stagecoach. Taverns provided accommodations which, although crude, served as social centers. By 1837, stage lines ran from Detroit as far west as Chicago, east to Buffalo, and north to Flint. The time to Chicago was four and a half days. The last of them were run from Detroit in 1873. Travel into the interior of the state was not possible until the military roads to Chicago and Fort Gratiot were built.

WESTERN STAGE CO.

Office, Woodward Avenue,
Corner of Jefferson Avenue.

Three daily Lines of Stages leave the office of the Western Stage company;—one via Ypsilanti, Tecumseh Jonesviile, White Pigeon, Niles, Michigan City to Chicago, through in four and a half days—one via Plymouth, Ann Arbor, Jacksonburgh, and Marshall to Kalamazoo, through in two days and a half—one via Monroe Toledo, Perrysburgh to Lower Sandusky, through in two days. Extras furnished on all of the above roads at the shortest notice.

JAMES L. GILLIS
Treasurer of the Western Stage Co.

TO EMIGRANTS.

At a respectable meeting of the citizens of

the vicinity of Mill-Creek, on the 19th inst. *Rufus Crossman* was called to the Chair, and *Samuel W. Dexter* chosen Secretary; the following resolutions were unanimously adopted.

1st—That we resolve ourselves into a society, to be called " *The Washtenaw County Society for the information of Emigrants;*" and that the citizens of the county be requested, to unite with us for the purpose of advancing the objects of this society.

2d—There shall be a President, Vice-President, Corresponding Committee, Secretary of the Corresponding Committee, and Secretary of the society.

3d—That all meetings of the society shall be called by the president or vice-president, and notified by the secretary of the society.

4th—That it shall be the duty of the secretary of the corresponding committee, to correspond with all societies in any part of the United States, who may apply for information respecting the soil, climate, local advantages &c. of the territory of Michigan, and the inducements which any portion of the country offers to emigrants; and generally, to answer all questions, and supply all information upon the subject of emigrating to this territory.

5th—That it shall be the duty of the secretary of the corresponding committee, to prepare a brief description of the territory of Michigan, and of the local advantages of the different sections of the territory; together with an address to the citizens of the United States, who may be disposed to emigrate to this country, and to publish the same in one or more papers of the territory.

6th—That Gov. Cass, be the president of this society; that Silas Kingsley, be the vice-president; that Messrs. **John Biddle, Jonathan Kearsley, John Mullett, Lucius Lyon, Sylvester Sibley, Orange Risdon, and Cyril Nichols,** be members of the corresponding committee; that Samuel W. Dexter be secretary of the corresponding committee, and secretary of the society, *pro tem.*

7th—That the preceding resolutions be published in the Detroit papers, with a request to printers in different parts of the United States to republish the same: and that a certain number of handbills to the same effect be struck off, and distributed abroad; and that it be the duty of the secretary of the society to carry this resolution into effect.

R. CROSSMAN, Ch'n.
S. W. DEXTER, Sec'y.

Mill-Creek, Washtenaw County, Feb. 19, 1827.   SHELDON & WELLS, Printers—*Detroit, Mich. Ter.*

A FORERUNNER OF CHAMBER OF COMMERCE promotion is this broadside designed to attract people to Michigan. For many years, the state paid special agents, even sent them to Europe to distribute literature and make contracts, in an effort to build up the population. At about the time of this resolution, Washtenaw County was populated by a large number of German farmers. (State)

He favored giving people in new states the right to vote on whether they wanted slavery or not. Zachariah Chandler, who emerged as a leader of the Michigan Republican Party which was founded under the oaks at Jackson in 1854, was closer to the feelings of the people, however, when he said, "Without a little blood letting, this Union, in my opinion, would not be worth a rush."

Michigan, which had proclaimed in its first constitution its desire to "encourage promotion of intellectual, scientific and agricultural improvement," also believed that "anti-slavery was righteousness," and as the Civil War approached, many of its people had demonstrated their feelings through support of the Underground Railroad and the Crosswhite case that developed at Marshall.

That event occurred in 1846 when Adam Crosswhite and his wife and four children, escaped slaves, were traced to Marshall where they had lived for two years, and were forcibly seized by deputies of their former owners in Kentucky. Crosswhite had fired a shot when they approached, a pre-arranged signal, and virtually the whole town showed up to grab the slave-hunters and order them to return to Kentucky. Crosswhite was freed and sent to Canada with his family.

Those who had aided Crosswhite—among them the leading families in the Marshall community—were sued by the former owner, found guilty, and assessed sizeable fines, but the incident sparked national attention and was one of many factors that led to passage of a new fugitive slave act which helped to precipitate the Civil War itself.

ON THE MORNING of June 6, 1822, Dr. William Beaumont, an army surgeon at Fort Mackinac, was called to treat Alexis St. Martin who had accidentally been shot in the stomach. The abdominal wound failed to heal, leaving an opening through which the stomach could be seen. Dr. Beaumont, prevailing on St. Martin to cooperate, fed him various foods over a period years in order to watch the course of digestion. In 1833, Dr. Beaumont wrote the book, *Experiments and Observations on the Gastric Juices and the Physiology of Digestion* which earned him worldwide acclaim. St. Martin, the man with the lid on his stomach, remained healthy, married, and lived to age seventy-six. This painting is by Dean Cornwall, and Beaumont's home is a museum on Mackinac Island today. (Free Press)

ANOTHER YOUNG MAN of talent who played a big part in Michigan's early history was Douglass Houghton. He was a physician, the first dentist to practice in Michigan and a professor of chemistry, geology, and mineralogy at the university. He served as mayor of Detroit in 1842 during which term the first public schools were established. In 1831, he accompanied Henry Schoolcraft on a trip to the Ontonagon River, and chipped a piece off the famous copper boulder found there earlier. In 1837, he became the state's first geologist, and undertook a thorough survey of mineral resources. His 1841 report helped trigger the copper rush that came a few years later, and in 1844, while surveying near Negaunee, his party discovered great amounts of exposed iron ore. Houghton, only thirty-six, drowned in 1845 when the small boat he was in capsized on Lake Superior during a storm. (DHM)

HOW SURVEYORS marked trees to indicate precise locations. (Houghton)

[38]

BURT'S SURVEYING COMPANY, with Marquette in the distance: On September 19, 1844, William A. Burt, a deputy surveyor, pinpointed a rich iron ore deposit where Negaunee stands today. This helped to speed building of the Soo locks, and by 1890 Michigan was the country's leading iron-ore producer. However, the lead lasted only until the discovery of ranges in Minnesota. Burt, also the inventor of the solar compass, was part of a surveying party working with Douglass Houghton when he noted that his magnetic compass was acting up. It developed, of course, that the ore field caused the deviation.

So Michiganians stood for principle—and as the pre-war period ended, they had also achieved some material progress. Frame houses were replacing the log cabins as saw mills sprang up. There was carpeting and improved furniture, and stoves to provide better heating and cooking facilities. The general health and welfare was improved with new waterworks, better fire protection, and even street lighting in the larger cities such as Detroit, Grand Rapids, and Kalamazoo.

The momentum that finally began to build up with the great surge of the 1830s thus put Michigan in a position to provide men and materials for the Civil War—and the boom would continue through and after the war.

It would build to a crescendo in the decades after 1865, and when mining and lumbering began to fade as key factors in the economy, the 1890s would see the emergence of a new industry built on the fortunes and the skills that had been accumulated earlier.

By 1890, the state's population would finally reach 2,093,889, and Hazen S. Pingree would emerge as the first of the major progressive leaders who would keep appearing on the Michigan scene at regular intervals, as the state's population would double and double again by 1970.

The state, which one man in 1812 saw as merely a "den for Indians and Traitors," was by 1890 the home of the nation's most diversified collection of peoples, each providing an important ingredient to the culture and the skills needed for the industrial and social revolutions of the twentieth century.

[39]

THE ONTONAGON BOULDER, first seen by Alexander Henry in 1766, was rediscovered in 1820 when Schoolcraft accompanied Gen. Lewis Cass on his territorial tour. The huge nugget of pure copper—70 inches long, 41 inches wide, and 18 inches thick—now rests in the Smithsonian Institution. Finding the great copper mass on the bank of the Ontonagon River, Henry started mining after fleeing the Michilimackinac massacre. He stayed only a year. The copper rush beagn in earnest when hundreds swarmed into the Keeweenaw Peninsula from 1843 to 1845. Houghton was founded by Ransom Sheldon and C. C. Douglas, who also platted land on the opposite side of the Portage River in 1859, establishing Hancock.
(Houghton)

MOST FAMOUS OF ALL was the Cliff Mine. It was the first mine in the world ever to be opened on a vein bearing only copper in the natural state. The vein was discovered in 1845. (Houghton)

The foundations for such development had been well laid by imaginative and hardy pioneer-founders. Hundreds of stories can be told, but two will suggest the quality of their characters.

Out of the East, for example, came the Ketchum brothers, Sidney and George, and they christened their town Marshall in honor of the then-chief justice of the United States —and also because they wanted their town to be a great political and cultural center.

In fact, one citizen even built a governor's mansion that was never used because the Legislature voted to put the Capitol in Lansing instead.

And there were those like Marilla Nearpass who came from New York state when she was thirteen and married Samuel N. Bentley who lived in Bentley Corner, which is about seventeen miles southwest of Albion.

As she told it, "Pa bought a span of horses and a new covered wagon and started. Father got discouraged (as we had to come through the woods, there was no road) and wanted to go back but Ma and I teased him to go on, but he said that he would not so we turned and intended to go back to Rose. But we stopped at a tavern overnight and got rested and we teased Pa to come to Michigan until he consented to start once more . . ."

"We could get any price we wished for our team and wagon, so we sold them for three yokes of oxen, three plows, some flour, 10 sheep, some chickens, another old wagon, etc."

AS A BAPTIST MISSIONARY, the Rev. John Booth, produced this sketch of Grand Rapids in 1831. Three structures on the right made up Louis Campau's trading post, while the five cabins across the Grand River were on the Baptist mission ground. In the middle of the river is the north portion of Island No. 1, and the slope at right center is part of old Prospect Hill. (Grand Rapids)

MR. AND MRS. SAMUEL BENTLEY

LOUIS CAMPAU, seen here in 1865, helped to found Saginaw, and later also earned the name of "Father of Grand Rapids." The son of a prominent French family, he was born in Detroit in 1791, and started as a fur trader. By 1927 he had settled in Grand Rapids, building a log cabin and trading post there. He died in 1871. (Grand Rapids)

[41]

TITUS BRONSON located his town on the Kalamazoo River in 1831, named it for himself, but left only a few years later when people in the community changed its name to Kalamazoo. He was a native of Connecticut who had a reputation for eccentricity. (Gazette)

THE FIRST COURT SESSION held in Bronson (now Kalamazoo) is depicted by Anthony Cooley, an early resident. It was held in 1832, and shows Titus Bronson, founder of the community, seated at the left of the long table in the rear. (Gazette)

THIS WAS MICHIGAN in 1837 when the state was admitted to the Union. Detroit, the capital, had a population of 9,763, but most of the northern part of the state was still wilderness. (DHM)

CONGRESS OF THE UNITED STATES;

At the *second* Session,

Begun and held at the City of Washington, on Monday, the *fifth* day of December, one thousand eight hundred and *thirty-six*.

AN ACT

to admit the State of Michigan into the Union, upon an equal footing with the original States.

Whereas, in pursuance of the act of Congress of June the fifteenth, eighteen hundred and thirty-six, entitled "An act to establish the northern boundary of the State of Ohio," and to provide for the admission of the State of Michigan into the Union upon the conditions therein expressed," a convention of delegates, elected by the people of the said State of Michigan, for the sole purpose of giving their assent to the boundaries of the said State of Michigan as described, declared, and established, in and by the said act, did, on the fifteenth of December, eighteen hundred and thirty-six, assent to the provisions of said act, therefore:

Be it enacted by the Senate and House of Representatives of the United States of America in Congress assembled, That the State of Michigan shall be one, and is hereby declared to be one, of the United States of America, and admitted into the Union on an equal footing with the original States, in all respects whatever. Section 2. And be it further enacted, That the Secretary of the Treasury, in carrying into effect the thirteenth and fourteenth sections of the act of the twenty third of June, eighteen hundred and thirty-six, entitled "An act to regulate the deposites of the public money," shall consider the State of Michigan as being one of the United States.

Speaker of the House of Representatives.

Vice President of the United States, and President of the Senate.

approved this 26th January 1837 —

Andrew Jackson

THEN CAME STATEHOOD. When the 1834 census showed that Michigan had 85,856 people, Stevens T. Mason, the young acting governor, pushed for faster action towards statehood. A constitutional convention was called for May 1835, and finally in December, Congress adopted an act making Michigan the 26th state in the Union. It was approved on January 26, 1837, by Pres. Andrew Jackson.

A FASCINATING PART of Michigan history is the story of its boy governor, Stevens T. Mason. The son of Gen. John T. Mason of Kentucky who was appointed secretary of the territory in 1830, Stevens helped his father and became well acquainted with his work. Stevens had impressed Gov. Lewis Cass enough that when his father resigned in the summer of 1831, Pres. Andrew Jackson granted Cass' request that the son replace him. The young Mason ran into strong opposition, but finally won, and took his oath as secretary on July 24, 1831. When Cass resigned as governor and George Porter replaced him, only to die in July 1834, Mason became acting governor and was elected to the job when statehood (which he had strived for) was won. By 1839, however, since he had become unpopular because of the panic of 1837 and a bank scandal, he became embittered and declined to run again. He moved to New York where he died in 1841 at age thirty-five. (DHM)

AND THIS WAS DETROIT at the same time, seen from the vantage point of the river front and from Windmill Point on the far east side. (Free Press-Ford)

TYPICAL OF NOTES produced when wildcat banks flourished in Michigan in the late 1830s is this one by the Bank of Pontiac in 1835. The State Legislature had enacted what were considered democratic laws for banking, one providing groups of twelve or more men to set up a bank without a special state charter. Since Michigan banks could issue notes that could pass as currency, when a second law relieved them of having to pay out coins for the notes, it opened doors to wildcat banks producing a flood of notes that eventually proved worthless. After things were brought in control, by 1845, only three banks survived, and they operated under special state charters. (Burton)

THE FIRST STATE CAPITOL was built in Detroit in what is now Capitol Park in the heart of the downtown section. It was later used as a school when a new capitol was built in Lansing, after the legislature had voted the move in 1847. At that moment, there wasn't even a log cabin at the site "in the township of Lansing in the County of Ingham" which the legislature had selected, but a building was erected, and the legislature met in the new town in 1848. (Free Press)

KALAMAZOO COLLEGE was Michigan's first denominational school, organized in 1831. Known as the Michigan and Huron Institute, it was chartered and incorporated in 1855 as Kalamazoo College. Always strong in promoting education, Michigan committed itself early to a major institution, the University of Michigan, founded in Detroit in 1817. It was later moved to Ann Arbor in 1841 because a local land company offered forty acres free, to attract the school. The legislature established Michigan State Normal School at Ypsilanti in 1853, and opened the Michigan Agricultural College in 1857 as the first state agricultural college in the United States. The picture shows Kalamazoo campus about 1860. (State)

THE LUTHERANS who had founded Frankenmuth three years earlier, established this mission of Bethany near St. Louis in 1848. Religious zeal proved to be a major driving force for many who came to Michigan. In a history of the period, Herman F. Zehnder wrote that Chief Bemassikeh, a Chippewa, told the founders, "Teach my people the truth." This sketch was made by a missionary in 1852. (Frankenmuth)

WILLIAM HOWLAND CRAPO left New Bedford, Massachusetts, where he was a leading businessman and public figure, to come in 1856 to the frontier town of Flint, population 2,000. He came because he was heavily committed in Michigan's lumber business, and most of his family followed him reluctantly in 1858. In time, Crapo operated three lumber mills, built the first railroad to the city, became its mayor in 1860, and governor of Michigan in 1864. His daughter Rebecca, second from right, second row, married William Clark Durant, and was the mother of William Crapo Durant, who later put together General Motors. The Crapo saga of Yankee ingenuity was repeated many times in Michigan history. (Journal)

CHARLES T. HARVEY, a young man summering in Sault Ste. Marie for his health in 1852, was aware of the potential of the copper and iron ore mines and he acted quickly after Congress approved building the Soo Locks. He convinced his employers, the Fairbanks Scale Company, of the project's feasibility, and they took the lead in getting the job underway. Harvey, who later (when this picture was taken) helped build the first elevated railroad in New York, was on hand when the Soo marked the fiftieth anniversary of the locks in 1905. (Burton)

BEFORE THE LOCKS, boats on skids were moved along these rails to get them around the rapids of the St. Mary's River. The view is of Sault Ste Marie's Water Street in 1850, looking east. (Soo)

A MAJOR BREAKTHROUGH came in 1852 when Michigan finally won Congressional approval to build a canal and locks at Sault Ste. Marie. Because Lake Superior is twenty-two feet above Lake Michigan and Lake Huron, and a rapids is part of the connecting St. Mary's River, cargo had been portaged for years. But discovery of iron ore and copper in the Upper Peninsula made building a canal critical. Digging began on June 4, 1853. By May 1855, the contractors were finished, having used 3,157 kegs of powder in the process of blasting out the canal. (Burton)

[49]

"ALMOST ANYTHING except a lodging might be bargained for" at this market, according to Silas Farmer, Detroit historian. It was located behind City Hall in what is now Cadillac Square and, added Farmer, "thrifty ladies, making selections with fastidious care, swelled the throngs, and younger ladies, in their morning walks, here found zest and perchance a beau." The market eventually moved farther east, but even in the late 1800s, butchers were still selling at one end of the square. (DHM)

HOUSE & LOT
FOR SALE.

THE FRAME HOUSE in that improving locality, corner of Third and Larned Streets, near the New Depot, is now for sale.

Persons desirous of investing money in a safe way can apply on the premises, to

JOHN O'FLYNN.

Detroit, July 6, 1848.

Corner of Third & Larned Sts.

AS THE WAR APPROACHED: Two people, Sojourner Truth and Zachariah Chandler, symbolized Michigan's role in the Civil War as the state showed signs of major growth.

DETROIT WAS EXPLODING into the suburbs—all the way out to Third and Larned when real estate man John O'Flynn posted this notice on one of the houses he had for sale. (DHM)

SLAVE, MILITANT, LECTURER, underground railroader, friend of Abraham Lincoln—all of these aptly describe Sojourner Truth who spent a good part of her life in Battle Creek. For many in Michigan an inspiration, she was actively involved in the abolitionist movement after she was freed in New York in 1827. Of her name she said, "The slave takes the name of her master. My master is the Almighty and his name is Truth; I'm a sojourner on this earth so I call myself Sojourner Truth." Battle Creek was a key spot of the underground railroad that moved escaped slaves to freedom, many into Canada. Sojourner was 105 years old when she died in 1883, and is buried in Battle Creek. (State)

[51]

ZACHARIAH CHANDLER was another New Englander who came to Michigan at age twenty and became thoroughly involved. He was born in New Hampshire, arrived in Detroit in 1833, and became a wholesale dry goods merchant. In 1851, he was elected mayor of Detroit, made one unsuccessful bid for the governorship, and was elected United States senator in 1857 to succeed Lewis Cass, serving until 1881. A strong anti-slavery advocate, he was considered a major power in the state's Republican party and was present when it was formed in 1854 in Jackson. (Burton)

NEWS OF THE FIRING on Fort Sumter which proved to be the signal for the beginning of the
Civil War, brought out one mass gathering after another in downtown Detroit in April 1861. Speeches
were made, flags were raised, and at one point in a meeting at City Hall 3,000 children sang "The Star
Spangled Banner." The crowd shown here was gathered in front of the U.S. Customs and Post Office
building, affirming its resolve by taking the pledge of allegiance en masse. (Burton)

MICHIGAN SOLDIERS took part in hundreds of battles, and 13,985 lost their lives during the Civil War, so it was not surprising to see a huge turnout on August 2, 1861, when the state's First Regiment, veterans of Bull Run, returned home. The crowd gathered at Detroit's Brush Street station, and they even stood on adjoining box cars to greet the men. (Burton)

LATER, THEY JAMMED the area for a stirring speech by Judge Charles I. Walker. (Burton)

MICHIGAN'S THIRD CAVALRY represented communities in the southern part of the state, and these men served as blacksmiths for the unit. Top row (left to right) John H. Askin, Kalamazoo; John Basler, Port Austin; Hiero B. Fox, Gratiot County; Nelson Hinds, Ionia; and George Clinton, Pinckney. Front row: Loammi Crowell, Tecumseh; J. Smith; John Priest, Bloomingdale; Andrew Bassford, St. Joseph; William Eakam, Jackson; and Lewis B. Rubel, Watervliet. (Free Press)

THIS WAS WHAT REMAINED of the flag of Michigan's 24th Regiment in the Civil War after it fought in the Battle of Gettysburg. Its losses in that one engagement were 339 men killed, wounded, and missing. (Free Press)

AND YET ANOTHER great multitude gathered in Campus Martius on April 25, 1865, for memorial services honoring Pres. Abraham Lincoln, who had been killed ten days earlier. (Burton)

The Bountiful Land

AS THE POST-WAR ERA started, signs of growth showed throughout the state. Two views of Detroit, one showing the skyline from the Windsor side with sidewheelers at the docks and the other showing a ferry boat heading across the river to Detroit, give one the feel of this. A closeup map of Flint in 1867, *(facing page)* suggests similar development there, where the population was approaching 3,000, primarily because of the sawmills on the Flint River, in the foreground. (Dowling-Journal)

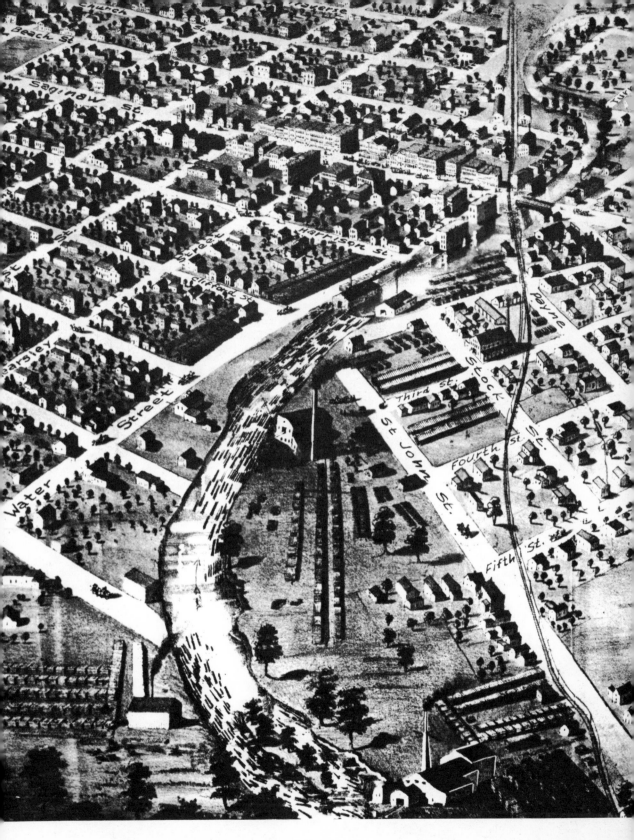

REGARDED BY MANY as a joke when first proposed as the state capital, Lansing began to emerge as a sizeable community by 1875 when construction was started on a new State Capitol. In 1847, after bitter controversy in which Detroit, Ann Arbor, Jackson, and Marshall made strong bids, the legislature picked Lansing because of its central location and, even in those days, because of the legislature's negative feelings towards the big city. (State)

AND FINALLY, here is a view looking down Michigan Avenue at the completed building. (State)

A UNIVERSITY OF MICHIGAN party, meanwhile, took a scientific look in 1868 at what was happening in the iron and copper mines of the Upper Peninsula. The expedition, led by Dr. Alexander Winchell, director of the university's museum, got as far as Isle Royale, of which one member in the group said: "No sooner had I cast my eyes around me than all my fatigue was forgotten. . . ." Seen here in Ontonagon County is the Evergreen Bluff copper mine that the group inspected. (Free Press)

OUT IN THE WILDERNESS in 1859 rose this Mt. Clemens railroad station, seen while construction on the road was still underway. What railroads meant to a community is demonstrated by the fact that in the late 1800s a fast freight came in from Baltimore in a day and a half or two. In contrast, in February 1839, an ad in a Detroit paper claimed unusual the fact that oysters were for sale which had arrived only 20 days from Baltimore. The Mt. Clemens station, between Port Huron and Detroit, was part of the Grand Trunk Railway which extended to Portland, Maine, and through Canada, and was the third road opened between Detroit and the East. (Ford)

[59]

IT STARTED FIRST on a large scale in the Saginaw Valley when a man named Harvey Williams set up a steam sawmill in 1834.

Great impetus for expansion came after a shipment of pine was made to the East in 1847 via the Great Lakes and the Erie Canal. People were impressed by the quality of the lumber, and in the years that followed, the flow from Michigan to help produce the houses and other buildings of the East increased to a point where there were 73 mills in the Saginaw Valley alone.

In the meantime, in the western part of the state, logs were floating down the rivers to Grand Rapids and Muskegon and, as 1860 started, there were mills scattered at the mouths of rivers along the northwest coast of Michigan and at Escanaba and Menominee in the Upper Peninsula.

For the next forty years, the lumbermen would dominate the economy of the state, building up fortunes while denuding the land, and by 1890 there were 1,957 sawmills producing more than four and a half billion board feet of lumber a year.

WHEN MICHIGAN MEANT lumber to the rest of the world: Something of the majesty of the forests that men attacked is captured in this cameo picture of two lumberjacks and a tree. (Ford)

OVER THE YEARS hundreds of pictures of lumber camps must have been taken by itinerant photographers. A. A. Bradbeer of Cadillac shot this one of the David Ward camp in Kalkaska County on February 18, 1844. The camps usually had a central kitchen and dining room building, and food consisted primarily of potatoes, beans, pork, bread, molasses, and strong tea. The bunkhouse usually held a series of double deckers, and other buildings accommodated carpenters, blacksmiths, and probably a small store. No liquor was allowed—but the men made up for it when they hit town in the spring. There's a lot of folklore about lumberjacks, but in any case they had to be tough and hardy to make it in the wilds. They sang a lot at night, and held boxing bouts to entertain each other. (Ford-State)

MOVING THE LUMBER required all sorts of equipment; the most dramatic were big wheels used to drag several logs at a time. Later there were cranes to lift logs onto railroad cars, and great sleds *(facing page, top)*, piled high to move millions of feet of lumber for trips to the mills. (Ford-Soo-State)

about 1907

THE BIG WHEELS, on occasions, were dressed up for celebrations at a nearby town. (Ford)

GREAT LOG JAMS were created as the trees came down the river to mills like the one below built by Henry Crapo in Flint in the 1870s. Eventually, most of the lumber, cut into various sizes, was loaded on ships, such as one shown at Boyne City *(facing page, top)*, to go to Chicago and to the East for the building of the cities of America. And there were kitchens for the boomers as shown on this picture *(facing page, bottom)* of logging on the Cass River near Frankenmuth (about 1900). (Frankenmuth-Journal-Smith)

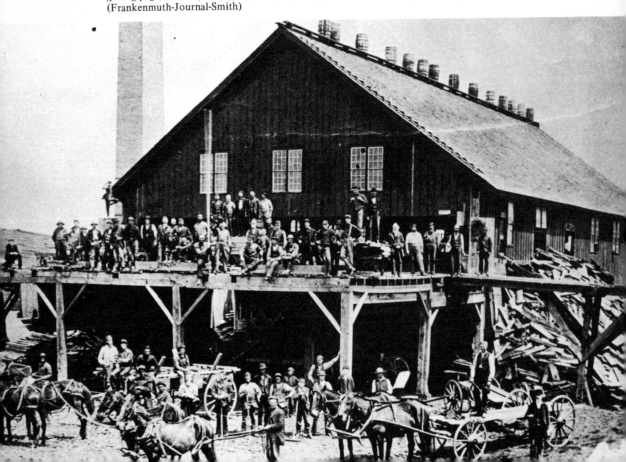

WHEN BOYNE CITY was a railroad and lumbering center, its waterfront was one of the busiest in Michigan. (Smith)

WHAT SEEMS LIKE a farewell party is this scene at an unidentified lumber camp which obviously, taking note of the Sunday-best dressed ladies and gentlemen, suggests some noteworthy occasion. Unfortunately, it seems like the end of a forest, based on the view of the surrounding land. (Ford)

THE NATIONAL CENTENNIAL was celebrated with vigor in 1876 as suggested by this great broadside calling attention to the celebration scheduled in Battle Creek. In the meantime, Michigan also was represented at the Philadelphia Centennial Expostition by this incredible bit of architecture—called Michigan House on the Avenue of States. It was designed to make use of every conceivable kind of lumber produced in Michigan, which was still in the heyday of lumbering at the time. (Enquirer-Marshall)

GRAND RAPIDS TOOK note of the nation's centennial by building an 86-foot-high arch from thousands of evergreen branches. (Grand Rapids)

THE LARGEST VILLAGE in the United States by 1884, when it received its city charter, Kalamazoo was already known for its manufacture of paper products, stoves, and pharmaceuticals. Kalamazoo was the name given the river by Indians because of nearby rapids which they suggested were a boiling pot *(kalamazoo)*. The scene above is looking west from Portage Street in 1876, a time when the city was illuminated by gas, which brings to mind Levi Benjamin *(right)*, who plied the gas-lighter trade at Maple Ridge. (Consumer-State)

THE GRAND RAPIDS and Indiana railroad helped to open up the western side of the Lower Peninsula for resorts, and one of the more elaborate ones developed at Harbor Springs where people in rockers sitting on the veranda could enjoy watching the golfers tee off. The Arlington Hotel *(below)* at Petoskey also attracted large contingents with its 100 rooms that included bathrooms, bowling rooms, and parlors. Two trains ran daily and, in addition, hundreds came by boat from Chicago. (Burton-Petoskey)

THE OAKLAND HOTEL in St. Clair was ideal for providing "proper amusement (as) a promoter of health," to read the promotion brochure. Its veranda, including bathhouses, was 800 feet long, and it boasted that its "Bath-Rooms are the finest bath-rooms in the United States." There were 30 of them— for mineral bath purposes, of course. Hundreds came by ships of the Star Cole and Red Star Line, including the steamer *Greyhound* shown unloading passengers on the St. Clair River. (Burton)

[71]

Detroit Charity Ball 1885. Thursday Eve. Feb. 5th. Detroit Roller Skating Rink. ISSUED TO Katie Hendrie

A BIG SOCIAL EVENT for Katie Hendrie in 1885 was the Detroit Charity Ball, held on February 5 at the Detroit Roller Skating Rink. To prove it, the back of the invitation turns out to be a program in which she listed the names of her partners for various events and dances that evening. (DHM)

[72]

UNIQUE AMONG RESORTS that developed was Bay View, an area adjacent to Petoskey and described as a moral place: "True, the vicious may come there, as they may go anywhere in the world. But the watchful care of the Association is exercised to keep the encampment as free from moral dangers to families who gather there as possible." Those words of the late 1880s hold true even today, since descendants of the early pioneers still live there. It was organized as a Methodist camp in 1875 when the original 325 acres were given to the association by the Grand Rapids and Indiana Railroad, which, in a sense, was trying to promote passenger business. One hundred years later, the association still owns the property and leases it to 800 members who occupy some 400-plus houses on the grounds, many built before the turn of the century. (Bay View)

AMONG THE FIRST to arrive at Bay View were these families and, typically, they gathered for camp meeting under the trees. A variety of ministers and speakers, including Frances Willard, founder of the Women's Christian Temperance Union, came to talk. By 1905, Bay View streets began to be crowded, although there was the occasional house standing alone that was an eye catcher such as the one at right. (Bay View-Petoskey)

WHEN THE CIRCUS came to Detroit in
the 1870s, the parade coming down
Grand River towards Woodward brought
out the kids—of all ages (Burton)

STUDENTS LITERALLY were helping to build their own boarding home—which they called Saint's
Rest—when Michigan's agricultural college opened for classes in 1857. Tree stumps were left to give
them some place to sit. Almost a score of years later, in 1874, the campus *(below)* still had that look
of wilderness about it. (MSU)

SOME INDIAN FAMILIES cluster beside the place they call home, while at another point in the Upper Peninsula, photographer B. F. Childs was getting this picture of Mrs. "Lo" and Little "Negee" which he entitled, "Indian Mother and Child." In 1870, Michigan's Indian population was still about 7,000, and many were located in areas that had been designated as reservations after the series of treaties earlier in the century.
(State)

CRITICAL FOR SHIPS plying the lakes between Buffalo and Chicago were the North and South Manitou Islands which in the mid-1800s developed into "wooding stations" for them. One of the first men to stop at Manitou was John Lerue who found that Nicholas and Simeon Pickard had established docks there. Lerue later went to the mainland and became the first white man to inhabit Leelanau County at what is now Glen Arbor. The Pickards were New Yorkers who came to the island in 1846. No other white people lived on the mainland between Manistee and Presque Isle in Lake Huron, except at Mackinaw. Leland was an Indian village with about 3,300 people, and the Indians used birch bark canoes to come out to the islands to buy goods. (Skillman)

PROBABLY NO SINGLE THING was more frightening in the 1800s than the cry of "Fire!" which came all to often in a world that used lumber almost exclusively for its buildings. Newaygo *(above)* was virtually leveled when a big fire hit it on April 29, 1883, but fortunately at about the same time, volunteers were able to contain another fire that struck on Muskegon's main street. (Muskegon)

A SPECIAL MOMENT was this one during the second annual fair at Millersburg. (State)

YOU NEEDED A TRAIN, a stage, and a boat to get around the Charlevoix area in the late 1800s. The trains from various sections came into Boyne Falls; from there you took a stage into Boyne City, where the Charlevoix, Boyne City, and East Jordan line *(below)* got you through what was Pine Lake into East Jordan or Charlevoix. Boyne City was also a center for shipping a lot of lumber through what is now Lake Charlevoix. (Ford)

ONE OF THE LARGER DRYDOCKS on the Great Lakes was this one at the foot of Orleans Street in Detroit, operated by the Detroit Drydock Company. Farther down the river, at Wyandotte, was another dock and ship-building facility which brought forth a great crowd on the day of this launching. (Dowling)

THE FIRST CLUBHOUSE of a women's organization was built for the Kalamazoo Ladies' Library Association in 1871. The organization had been founded in 1852, and Lucinda Hinsdale Stone, an original member from Kalamazoo, is considered by many the "mother of women's clubs in Michigan." Similar clubs were formed in Battle Creek, Grand Rapids, Detroit, and Jackson. The Michigan Federation of Women's Clubs was organized in 1895 at Bay View, outside Petoskey. A Michigan WCTU was functioning even before the national group adopted the name Women's Christian Temperance Union. (Burton)

WHAT LOOKS LIKE a giant beehive is a huge kiln used for smelting iron ore near Menominee. (State)

TRAIN WRECKS managed to draw crowds—obviously crowds that could take things in stride. One occurred on the Harbor Spring Road in 1896 when the engine apparantly tipped over and made an interesting background for a derby-bedecked gentleman and some friends. After a head-on collision between one train carrying a load of lumber and another in 1897 near a Michigan Central Line station at Kawkawlin, some gentlemen even got on top of the engine's roofs, while the photographer tried very hard *(below)* for a well-balanced, artistic picture. (Marshall-Petoskey)

IN THE COUNTRYSIDE near Port Huron there was the peace that comes with fishing or just sitting and watching the fishing, epitomizing what we call the "good old days." (Burton)

A LABOR DAY PARADE in Battle Creek in 1888 at Monument Square: Unions became a major economic factor during the 1860s, when the powerful Brotherhood of Locomotive Engineers was organized in Marshall, then a hub for the Michigan Central Line. On July 4, 1865, union workingmen held their first parade in Detroit, and in the 1870s and early 1880s the Knights of Labor, the first broadscope labor union in the country, was a factor in Michigan. By 1881, however, skilled workers turned to the American Federation of Labor. The first strike in which the National Guard was called out and Pinkerton men were used involved a Saginaw lumbermill strike over working hours in 1885. Michigan unions led in the fight for an eight-hour day. Average wages about that time were $300 a year for women, $400 for men. (Enquirer)

IN 1899, THE CARPENTERS of Muskegon took occasion during the Labor Day parade for a bit of nostalgia to dramatize their craft. Note that the building in the display is for sale, probably to be used as a playhouse for some lucky kids. (Muskegon)

AND SPEAKING of construction and carpentering, this house near the Soo is an excellent example of the hewn covering in home construction—and its occupants obviously were pretty proud of it. (Soo)

[84] A BIG DAY FOR MUSKEGON was the appearance of James G. Blaine, the Republican presidential candidate who spoke there in 1884. Farmers had to drive all night to get to town to hear him in those days before radio and television, and it made for an unusually festive affair. Blaine lost the election by a narrow margin to Grover Cleveland. (Consumer)

NO COMMUNITY worth its salt was without its band. In 1885, Leslie provided a novel twist with this all-girl group that contested with the boys for playing at church and school festivals and fairs. The uniforms were black dresses, voluminous folds of cloth swirling around the ankles, and broad-brimmed hats pinned firmly. In Ypsilanti, this concert band was caught in a more traditional pose, riding in a carriage during a parade. Detroit, at the time, had five brass bands that were able to provide music for military affairs, or for dancing waltzes, mazurkas, and you name it. (State-Ford)

TWO GREAT FIRES swept parts of the state. One almost upstaged the Chicago fire while the other helped launch the Red Cross. On October 8, 1871, when fire broke out in Chicago, flames also destroyed Holland, swept up into Manistee, and then moved across the state to Lake Huron. The summer had been hot and dry, and great winds blew that day. Some say that sparks may have been carried from Chicago across Lake Michigan to ignite the state's forests. Eighteen thousand families were left homeless. Ten years later, in September 1881, a fire swept through Lapeer, Tuscola, and Huron counties in which 125 lost their lives, with some people fleeing into Lake Huron for protection. For the Red Cross, this was the first major disaster it had to handle, and the way it did brought kudos to itself and to Clara Barton, who directed things. The accompanying picture is of another forest fire—in 1946 —but it shows what it must have been like in those nineteenth-century days. (Free Press)

THIS IDYLLIC SCENE BECAME an inferno too, when the town of Au Sable was destroyed in a blaze that also wiped out Oscoda in 1911. (Ford)

SPEAKING OF FIRES, here's a sample of the men and equipment that battled them in cities across the state in the 1880s.

GRACIOUS LIVING is epitomized in this photograph of the marshmallow roast which followed a dinner party at the home of the Daniel Sears Manns in 1895. Daughters Jessie and Mary Ida were entertaining guests in the authentic Victorian home built in 1883 in Concord, a few miles from Albion. The home is now part of the growing number of historic attractions open to the public in Michigan. (State)

AN UNUSUAL PANORAMA of Grand Rapids is provided by this picture. A clever photographer took two shots and pasted them together where the job printing plant and the bank adjoin. The scene is at Pearl Street and Monroe. The sixteen-story Grand Rapids National Bank building stands at this triangle today. (Grand Rapids)

PORT HURON was celebrating completion of the international railroad tunnel connecting it with Sarnia, Canada, when it put up what seems to be a standard thing of the good old days— a festive arch. For Port Huron *(facing page, bottom)* there were also excursion boats, and in the same picture one may also note a streetcar operating on the state's first electrically powered line.
(Burton-State)

BIG-LEAGUE BASEBALL was first played in Michigan in 1880. In 1887, the Detroit team won the world championship because the previous year it had managed to corral four of the best players available—Rowe, Richardson, Brouthers, and White. In 1889, however, the owners sold off their best players and gave up their National League franchise. Baseball came back in 1900 and, of course, really began to flourish with the arrival of Tyrus Cobb in 1905. The Tigers have always remained a major attraction for Michigan fans. (DHM)

THIS DETROIT SCENE catches traffic at Woodward and Michigan in the 1880s. The tower at the left, which reaches to a height of 190 feet was part of the system lighting the city's streets. (Ford)

FROM HORSE-DRAWN STREETCARS that appeared first in Detroit in 1863, the move was to electrified transport that tied the city to its suburbs through the Interurban lines, which in their turn faded as the automobile began to take over. Main Street in Rochester, looking south, had interurban service in the early twenties, but the first of the automobiles can be seen along the curbs. (State)

NO, IT'S NOT THE OLD WEST nor a village in Europe, but Mulliken, population 484. It and Middleville (population 1, 196 as of 1965) have changed a little since these pictures were taken in the late 1800s, but they still retain a rural quality. Mulliken *(above)* is just outside of Grand Ledge on the border of Eaton and Ionia counties, and Middleville is thriving just outside of Hastings in Barry County. (State)

[91]

IF ONE SEARCHES, one finds that in the history of every community there are one or two people who make a memorable impression, for whatever reason, good, bad, or otherwise. Louis "Big Louie" Moilanen was one of the Copper Country's men to remember: Louie reached a height of 8 feet, one inch; weighed 400 pounds; had 24-inch thighs; and a neck measurement of 18. He was born in Finland and came to America at age four with his parents who moved to the Houghton-Hancock area. His mother was slightly over 4 feet tall, his father 5 feet 9. He was in the Ringling Circus for a while, also ran a saloon in Hancock, and served a term as justice of the peace there. He died at twenty-eight in 1913. (Houghton)

[92]

IN KALAMAZOO, the city scavenger (the man in charge of cleaning privies) and his two assistants fitted the description of town characters, and served as object lessons. On the back of this picture, are the words: "If these three familiar characters in the history of Kalamazoo of thirty years ago, had attended Sunday School, what a different story could be told . . . Beginning immediately, Major C. A. McClellan urges your attendance at his Sunday School morning at 10 o'clock." It seems an un-Christian way to attack men who were doing an honorable—and much needed—job in the years when sewers were only a dream. (Gazette)

ANOTHER PERSONALITY worthy of attention in the turn-of-the-century period was the itinerant bear-trainer who brought his animals into town for street performances. In this instance, it happened in Manistique.

AT NOON ON February 19, 1890, equipment was perched perilously at the edge of a bridge *(top)* that was just beginning to take shape over the Manistee River. By May 6, it was completed, and the first train *(center)* was rolling over it. At another time, covered bridges sprang up around the state. This one at Fallasburg *(right),* built in 1862 at a cost of $400, was made out of Michigan white pine grown near Greenville. (Grand Rapids)

$5 FINE FOR RIDING OR DRIVING ON THIS BRIDGE FASTER THAN A WALK

LOOK ABOUT YOU and see Tahquamenon Falls *(above)*, the most spectacular of Michigan's 150 waterfalls, and the surging closeup of Bond Falls *(facing page)*. Both are in the Upper Peninsula. Tahquamenon, near Newberry, drops forty-eight feet on its way to Lake Superior. (AAA)

A Time to Shift Gears

AS MICHIGAN MOVED toward the last decade of the nineteenth century, and the coming of the automobile, its attention was focused on Hazen S. Pingree, who emerged as one of the first of the great modern reform leaders in the country. Pingree came to Detroit from Maine because he had met Detroiters in a prison camp during the Civil War and had been impressed with what he had heard. He got into the shoe business, and by 1890 was prospering in partnership with Charles H. Smith.

In 1889, he was prevailed on to run for mayor of Detroit as a Republican. He pulled one surprise by winning in the even-then heavily Democratic city, and then surprised his Republican supporters by advocating municipal ownership of the transit company and exposing widespread corruption in the government.

In 1896 he ran for governor and won, and for a period of two months was both governor and mayor, but the Supreme Court ruled he had to choose. He chose the governorship. Pingree won great favor for his reaction to the Panic of 1893 when he

moved strongly to help people and even sold a favorite horse to raise money for seeds for gardens.

HAZEN PINGREE WAS the darling of newspaper cartoonists, who showed him combining with the Salvation Army *(below)* to help promote the potato patches which were his trademark (comparable to the Victory Gardens of the future). Pingree was elected mayor as a Republican by 2,300 votes in 1889, and also launched the battle to bring Detroit's transit system under public ownership. (DHM-Free Press)

GOV. PINGREE & STAFF.
OFFICERS 31ST 32ND 33RD 34TH

COPYRIGHT 1898
STERLING & CO'S
DETROIT.

WHEN WAR WAS DECLARED against Spain after the sinking of the *Maine* in Havana harbor on February 15, 1898, Michigan was called on to supply five regiments of volunteers. They trained at Island Lake, and before they left, Governor Pingree appeared at the head of an impressive display on the grounds. Thereafter, the 33rd Regiment boarded trains and went to see action in Cuba. The 34th was also in Cuba, and the 31st pulled police duty there after the war. Two other regiments, the 32nd and 35th, saw action only in Southern camps. (Willard)

[97]

IN FLINT, when the boys came marching home, a great crowd awaited them at the station. (Journal)

STANDISH TOOK ON THE AIR of a great festival when the Soldiers' and Sailors' Encampment and band meet was held there in September 1900. Tents pitched near the railroad provided living quarters for the crowd, and the editor of the *Arenac Independent* wrote with great feeling,
"Old maids may forget their age, young men may forget their plighted words, but at Standish people will never forget the great crowds, the quaint old vets, the thrilling music of the assembled bands, nor the whirlwind of enthusiasm which pervaded the meeting, especially on the last day." (Forsythe)

PUBLIC ATTENTION was also being paid to the Grand Army of the Republic, which had annual encampments around the state that caused much excitement. This is an 1898 GAR parade in Muskegon. *Below,* crowds jam Monroe in Detroit during another GAR parade. (DHM)

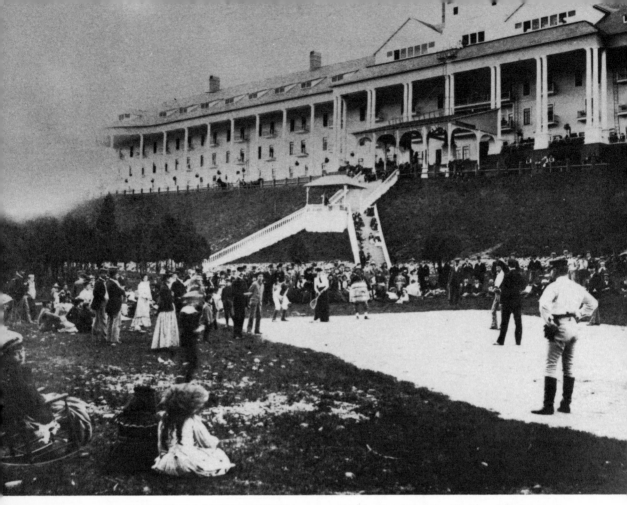

LARGEST OF ALL RESORT HOTELS in the world is the Grand Hotel on Mackinac Island opened on July 10, 1887. The land was originally purchased by Sen. Francis B. Stockbridge of Kalamazoo, who had made a fortune out of lumber. Additions made in 1897 and 1912 now bring the grounds of the hotel to 500 acres. Chauncey Depew was toastmaster for the opening dinner; among the guests were Mrs. Potter Palmer and a group of friends from Chicago who brought three hackney teams, saddlehorses, tallyhos, and carriages. From Detroit came Algers, Newberrys, Campaus, and Whitneys, and there were Swifts, Cudahys, and Armours from Chicago. One thousand guests a night jammed the hotel the first week it was opened. (Grand)

IT'S ONLY NATURAL that Michigan, with its water wonderland, is a center for much boating. Highlight of the year has been the annual race to Mackinac Island which always attracts some of the finest sailors in the country. In this 1903 view the yachts are at anchor after the race while their crews enjoy the delights of the taverns ashore. (Soo)

IT WAS STATE FAIR TIME in Detroit in 1894, and the kids were out in force. The fair, first held in 1848, was located roughly in the area now occupied by Wayne State University. (DHM)

WHEN WINTER CAME, people resorted to sleds, cutters, and even massive street rollers to help them get around. Front Street in Monroe had more than its share of horse-drawn sleighs on this winter day. (State)

IN CALUMET they brought out this huge roller to level off things. They needed six teams of horses and six drivers to get the job done. (Ford)

FEW INSTITUTIONS in Michigan have brought greater glory to the State over the years than the University of Michigan, which established its pre-eminence among all universities after 1850. And by 1909, when James Burrill Angel completed his remarkable 38-year stint as President, the University had grown to more than 5,000 students, with a distinguished faculty of more than 400. Academically, it was one of the finest anywhere, and in the early 1900s it also built a reputation as Champion of the West athletically. It was a time when Fielding H. Yost moved into leadership and the University of Michigan team was invited to the West Coast for the first Rose Bowl game in which it defeated Stanford, 49 to 0.

ANN ARBOR ITSELF was beginning to grow into a sizeable community as this view from the railroad bridge attests. (Burton)

CULTURE WAS IMPORTANT TOO. In 1894, the University launched what was to become a traditional May festival by bringing the Boston Symphony on campus for a performance in University Hall. (Burton)

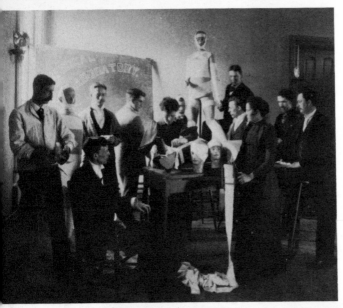

WOMEN APPEARED on campus in 1871 when Madelon Stockwell passed the entrance examination and enrolled, much to the disgust of many students and faculty. That feeling wore off, however, and by the 1890s women were participating in surgical laboratories. (State)

WORKING ON CADAVERS, students wore white, but somehow the hoped-for antiseptic look fails to come off in this corner of the dissecting room of the medical school. (State)

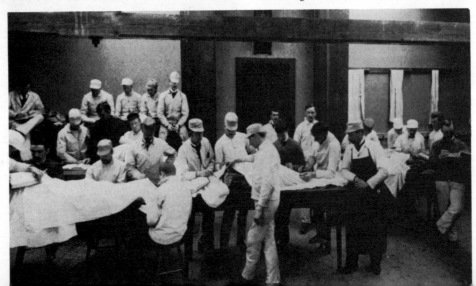

A SPOT COMPARABLE to today's Pretzel Bell, a local student hangout, was jammed in about 1907 with this hearty group of serious-looking seniors who are about to be—or have been—graduated. (Burton)

THE UNIVERSITY OF MICHIGAN routed Stanford in the first Rose Bowl game in 1902. One of the formations that helped is seen here. Stanford gave up before the end of the second half because of the bruising punishment. The score was 49 to 0. (State)

Weeks, Shorts, Snow, Heston, Herrnstein

TACKLE-BACK-RIGHT PLAY.

THIS STUDENT'S ROOM in the early 1900s has the busy look that seems typical of students' rooms in all ages. (Burton)

MEANWHILE, QUARTERS FOR COEDS at Michigan State in East Lansing had all the amenities one might expect for gracious ladies at the turn of the century. What was that, however, about women's liberation coming in the 1960s and 1970s? They were parading at MSU in 1921. The first women, ten of them, were admitted to MSU in 1870, the same year that U. of M. accepted them. By 1900 they were studying chemistry, botany, horticulture, floriculture, trigonometry, surveying, and bookkeeping among other things. (MSU)

THRESHING ON THE SEBASTIAN FARM outside of Albion about 1910 catches some of the drama of the Michigan farm effort first concentrated in the southern counties and essentially designed to serve the needs of the local population. But as the lumbermen moved north, the farmers followed, and began to grow enough to sell outside of Michigan. Wheat was the primary crop, and gradually corn, oats, barley, buckwheat, and hay were added, making Michigan a leader among the states in the value of agriculture. As years went by, other vegetables and fruits were produced, fitting the varied quality of soils. By 1950, the state still rated among the top five in value of agricultural products. (Albion)

A FEW YEARS LATER, science had produced the first calf by artificial insemination at Michigan State University. Shown in the MSU dairy barn about 1941 are Joseph Sykes, physiologist *(left)* and Lane A. Moore, specialist in animal research. (MSU)

[107]

THE CORNERSTONE-LAYING CEREMONY of Detroit's new High school in the early 1900s attracted a sizable crowd. Located at Cass and Warren, Central High was later to become the first building of Wayne State University but, at this time, appropriate provisions were made to accommodate younger students with a bicycle room in the basement. (Wayne)

THE UNIVERSITY of Detroit in the early 1900s planned on building a four-story, block-long edifice on East Jefferson, which somehow was featured in postcards of the day. The one that was actually built *(above)* was impressive but nor quite as massive. U of D was founded by the Jesuits in 1876, and over the years its students and graduates have played major roles in the social and political life of Michigan, as evidenced by some names in this group of pre-university students *(below)* at the turn of the century: Rabaut, Van Antwerp, Brennan, Maher, and Schiappacasse. By the 1920s the campus had been shifted to McNichols Road. (U. of D.)

HAVING MET IN A CONTEST OF BASEBALL police officers of Saginaw and Bay City posed in Bay City in the nineties with Saginaw's proud mascot taking the spot front and center. (News)

A GRAND RAPIDS CROWD on a Sunday in 1905 enjoyed watching workmen putting together the *Grand,* a stern-wheeler. Because of a time limit, the Sunday work was required, but an itinerant photographer obviously caused a slight delay in the schedule to arrange this impressive pose. (Grand Rapids)

THIS HOUSEBOAT was built for newsboys of the *Grand Rapids Press* shortly after it was organized in 1894. It took the boys on vacation cruises to Spring Lake. The newsboys also had a band, which may be seen playing as the houseboat is towed at the start of a trip. (Grand Rapids)

FLOODS, FIRES, AND WIND have often made
themselves felt in the state—leaving behind destruc-
tion—such as this cyclone that hit Owosso on
November 11, 1911. (State)

THE SAGINAW FLOOD OF 1904 loosened
the cedar-block pavement of the streets, and
gave a man and a boy a chance to float on a
plank. On East Genesee Street, boards were
placed on wooden horses so people could pro-
ceed about their business. (State)

[111]

MANY SURROUNDING BUILDINGS at the Superior Street bridge in Albion collapsed into the river during the flood of 1908. They almost hide the bridge, which also collapsed. (Albion)

SITTING AMONG THE RUBBLE, a woman tries to pick out her belongings after a cyclone tore apart her home in Fowlerville on May 15, 1909. (State)

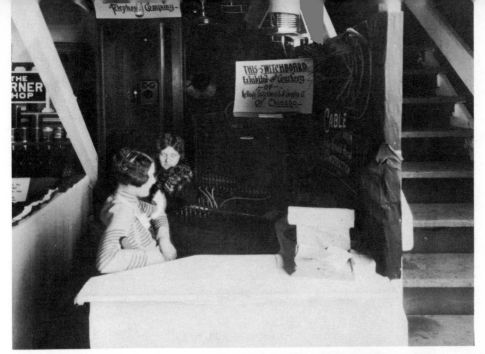

TELEPHONES WERE NOVELTIES enough to merit a special exhibit at the county fair in the early 1900s, and, by observing the layout and employes in the General Telephone Company's offices at South Haven about 1910 and at an insurance company in Detroit, one senses that offices in general had an air of formality, to say the least. In 1847, the first telegraph in Michigan was put up between Ypsilanti and Detroit along the Michigan Central tracks. The telephone, already demonstrated at the Philadelphia Centennial Exposition, was first used in Michigan in 1877 between a drugstore and a laboratory owned by Frederick Stearns. After patents expired in 1893, hundreds of independent telephone companies developed. (General-DHM)

LONG HAIRED BOYS
PLAY BALL.

House of David,
Base Ball Park

House of D

THE HOUSE OF DAVID, a religious organization founded by Benjamin F. Purnell at Benton Harbor in 1903, has created quite a stir through the years. It operates a summer resort built by the services and labor of members, whose long hair and beards were the sign of the House of David. These men won attention with a better-than-average baseball team, and with their stand as conscientious objectors during World War I. Today, House of David is a major Benton Harbor enterprise, owning and operating a cold-storage plant, a printing establishment, machine shops, greenhouses, and farms *(see also facing page)*. (State)

AINISTRATION BUILDINGS.
HOUSE OF DAVID.

THE HOUSE OF DAVID 1906

THERE WAS AN AIR of the personal touch to business as transacted around the state, and proprietors and employes alike seemed anxious, at a moment's notice, to drop everything and have their pictures taken. An era is revived in this brief look at how Michigan did its business and worked in the late 1890s and early 1900s.

THE DUFFANY BROTHER'S BAZAAR would put today's flea market to shame with the assortment offered to its Jackson customers. (Citizen)

THESE PEOPLE OF FRANKENMUTH were busy barreling apples in about 1900. Frankenmuth, still well known today for its German atmosphere, was built up by predominantly German immigrants who came to farm.

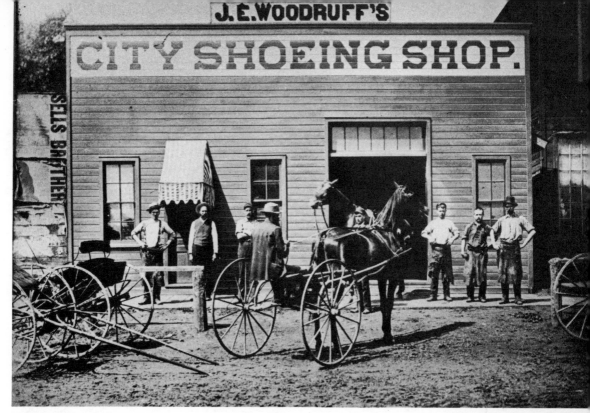

BEFORE THE AUTOMOBILE'S
arrival, Woodruff's City Shoeing Shop in
Jackson brought its employes out for
this pleasant turn-of-the-century photo.
(Citizen)

THIS MERCHANDISE DISPLAY
featured in the early 1900s at the
Washington Market in Marshall might
send today's health inspectors into fits
of screaming. (Marshall)

Sad End to an Era

THE BOOM ERA'S exciting developments began to fade in the Copper Country after the turn of the century, and a strike and a tragedy provided a sad anticlimax in 1913.

Until that time, a paternalistic management and a work force of primarily immigrant labor had lived in relative peace and prosperity. Organizing efforts had started in 1909, and the strike issue finally came when mine owners ordered the use of one-man drills, which were seen as another step towards reducing the number of jobs available.

Charles H. Moyer, president of the Western Federation of Miners, was there to lead the fight, and on July 23 some 16,000 miners and smelters were idled.

Things quickly became ugly, and the National Guard was called out, but miners began drifting back to work and calm returned. Then on Christmas Day, the death of 74 people, including 56 children at a Christmas party provided another stunning and anticlimatic blow to the area.

Facing page: LOOK ABOUT YOU and enjoy the view of Houghton Falls, which in this case is embellished by the efforts of a photographer who was trying to artistically pose man against the natural background. (Houghton)

IN COPPER COUNTRY in the late 1800s there was Houghton (left) and Hancock, two booming cities that have today settled into centers of a pleasant college-resort area. (DHM)

IN THE TAMARACK MINE near Houghton in 1892, these miners were using a drilling machine that required at least two men to set up. The mine owners later ordered a lighter drill to be handled by one man, thereby creating an issued that triggered the strike of 1913. (Houghton)

[122]

THESE OSCEOLA MINERS are being carried down a modest distance to a copper mine on this 1896 day. There would come a time when copper would be brought up from shafts that reached the incredible depth of 9,000 feet on the incline, or about 6,400 feet straight down. (Houghton)

OSCEOLA MINERS IN CAGE
1896

THE 1913 STRIKE in Houghton even had children enlisted in the parades. (Houghton)

A HOUGHTON SCHOOL GROUND was turned into an encampment for National Guardsmen. (Houghton)

THE ITALIAN HALL in Calumet above the A & P store was the scene of a happy Christmas party in 1913—when someone yelled "Fire!" In the rush that followed, bodies were piled up on the staircase leading down, inside the door at the left of the building. (Houghton)

THE HALL ITSELF was left in shambles by the surging crowd. (Houghton)

FISHING AND BASKETING-WEAVING provided a living for many Indians. In the photograph below, Indian women of the Chippewa tribe are making splint baskets at their home near Saginaw in 1894, while farther north at the rapids of the St. Mary's River *(above),* Indian men battle the turbulent waters in search of fish. (State)

THE BICYCLE was the "in" thing of the day during the 1880s and 1890s, and people rode them alone, in tandem, in races, and for trips of all kinds. The women in the group are from the Tawas area and are comparing notes after having reached the lifesaving station at Tawas Point on their outing in August 1897. (Osgood)

MORE SEDENTARY LADIES were those of the Fresh Air Society who took time to escort some youngsters for an outing at Detroit's Belle Isle in 1905. (UCS)

SCORES OF PEOPLE came from Grand Rapids and Kalamazoo to listen to then-Maj. William McKinley make a presidential campaign speech from his front porch in Canton, Ohio. Incredibly, McKinley attracted over a million people to his house that year. On this day, October 17, 1896, fifty trains had carried twenty-five delegations to Canton. The Grand Rapids delegation was escorted to the train by the drum corps of the United Workmen. (Grand Rapids)

[127]

POLITICS AND POLITICIANS have always managed to create more than a little interest in Michigan, but the pre-television days called for some imaginative approaches. For an 1895 Republican rally in Coldwater, local supporters arranged for a giant arch to be built on the main street, while in Detroit in about 1910, banners flew to advertise a (William) Taft Republican club excursion. (State-Burton)

THE BIGGEST MAN ever to be president—he weighed over 300 pounds and stood 6 feet tall—William Howard Taft made an appearance at Battle Creek on September 21, 1911. On the platform at the Michigan Central station that day an unusual number of prominent citizens of Battle Creek were present. The speech was considered part of a reelection campaign at a time when Theodore Roosevelt was about to launch his Progressive party. In 1912, Taft and Roosevelt lost to Woodrow Wilson. (Willard)

[129]

SOME VACATIONERS gather around while the musicians who played for dances at the Crystal Lake resort hall early in the century pose for a daytime picture. (State)

HAILED AS "the biggest inland . . . steamer in the world" when it was being built, the *City of Cleveland* attracted a huge crowd to the docks at Cheboygan when it arrived on June 6, 1908. On board were members of a cruise arranged by the Detroit Board of Commerce. The cruise, an annual event for years, has recently been held in the South. (Dowling)

RARE DRAMA IS CAPTURED in this picture showing the freighter *Utica* standing by and pumping water into the burning Rushmere Club on the St. Clair River. The unusual incident occurred on August 28, 1908, and the effort, while noteworthy, was not enough to save the building from being gutted. The Rushmere was only one of many resorts that drew thousands to the St. Clair flats during the summer months. (Dowling)

ORGANIZED BY a group of doctors, lawyers, musicians, and businessmen in 1897, the Iroquois Club became a major social organization for blacks in Michigan. It owned two buildings at Antoine and Beacon in Detroit, using one with fifteen rooms for a clubhouse while renting the other. Here in 1910, they had gathered to participate in a memorial event for Frederick Douglas. (Burton)

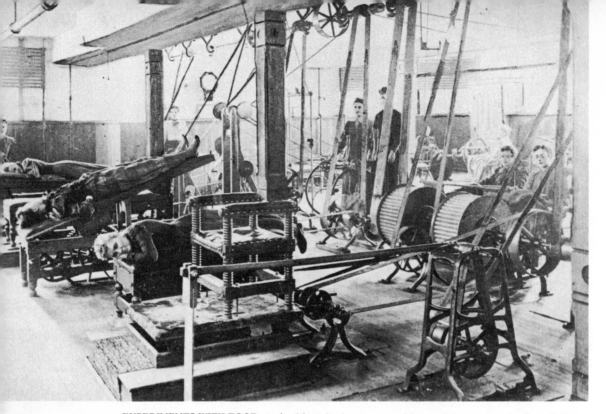

EXPERIMENTS WITH FOOD at a health sanitarium sponsored by a religious group, the Seventh Day Adventists, triggered the idea for one of Michigan's largest industries and made Battle Creek the "Cereal Bowl of the World." Dr. John Harvey Kellogg became superintendent of the Health Reform Institute, which he renamed the Battle Creek Sanitarium. The Seventh Day Adventists, strong advocates of vegetarianism, attacked the evils of over-eating and over-drinking. The "San" became a mecca for health-seekers. It provided them with exercise machines of infinite variety *(above)* and outdoor dancing sessions on the patio after a new building replaced the original one destroyed by fire. Dr. Kellogg himself developed eighty new grain and nut products to use at the "San," and he greatly extended previous experiments with flaking cereal grain. Noting this his younger brother, William K. Kellogg, launched a business. C. W. Post, a patient, decided on a commercial venture in the field, too, developing a drink called Postum, and Grape Nut Cereal which he first called Elijah's Manna. Post also developed the advertising techniques that helped spread the news worldwide. (Willard)

THE ORIGINAL SANITARIUM *(above)* was later replaced by a brick skyscraper that boasted a patio on which dance sessions were held as part of the therapy. The brochure tells of all the wondrous things that happened at the sanitarium. (Willard)

MEDICAL — SANITARIUM AND — SURGICAL

Turkish, Russian, Roman, Solar, Electric, Thermo-Electric, Electro-Vapor, and All Kinds of Water Baths, Swedish Movements by Machinery and administered by trained Manipulators, Massage, Pneumatic Treatment by means of Compressed and Rarified Air, Vacuum Treatment, Etc. The Swedish Movement Department is the Most Complete in the United States.

ALL FORMS OF ELECTRICITY are employed, including the recently revived Statical Electricity. Special attention given to the treatment of Dyspepsia, Diseases of Women, Diseases of the Eye, Ear, Nose, Throat, and Lungs, and to Surgical Cases.

"It is the best Sanitarium I know of."—*Wendell Phillips.*
"In all my travels I have found none that equals it."—*Mrs Mary L. Livermore.*
"It is superior to any in my acquaintance."—*Prof. A. Bronson Alcott.*

This institution is universally acknowledged to be the most complete and thoroughly rational and scientific establishment for the treatment of the sick in the United States, and probably in the World.

Send for Circulars.   *Address,* SANITARIUM, Battle Creek, Mich.

THIS BUILDING was where W. K. Kellogg turned out his first boxes of cereal. Eventually, the plant grew and white-frocked employes *(below)* did the packing. (Enquirer)

"SWEETHEART OF THE CORN" was featured on early Kellogg Corn Flake boxes. (Enquirer)

[134]

AUCTIONS ALWAYS managed to draw a crowd, and this one in the middle of the street in Standish *(above)* was no exception. Meanwhile in Albion, a farmer put together his own broadside, which gives some idea of the scope of farming in that period. (Forsythe-Albion)

AUCTION SALE

Having decided to lease our farm, we will sell at public auction on the place three miles east of Albion on the territorial road, on

Friday, March 18th

Commencing at 10.00 o'clock sharp, the following property :

~ SIX HORSES ! ~

One nine-year-old sorral Gelding, weight 1200; 1 brown Mare 9 years old, weight 1200; 1 brown Gelding 5 years old, weight 1150; 1 bay Gelding 5 years old; wt 1100; 1 3-yr-old brown Mare; 1 brown Mare with Colt 7 months old, with foal by Cliftons coach horse.

13 Head of Cattle !

Two new milch Cows, calved Jan 1st, 8 and 6 yrs old; 2 calved Feb. 15th, 5 and 3 yrs old; 3 due to calf last of April, 8 and 3 yrs old; 1 Cow farrow, 6 yrs old; 5 head of young cattle.

ELEVEN HOGS 2 brood Sows, 1 due to farrow April 1st, 9 Shoats.

Farm Implements These tools are all nearly new and in first-class condition. 2 Champion Binders, one nearly new, 1 Deering Mower, 1 Empire Grain Drill, 1 10½ foot Hay Rake, 1 pivot-axle riding Cultivator, 2 set of Binder Trucks, 1 Land Roller, 2 spring Drags, one nearly new, 2 steel-beam Plows, 1 99 Oliver Plow, 1 15A Gale Plow, 1 8-tooth Cultivator, 1 canopy-top Surrey, 1 top Buggy, 2 Buggy Poles, 1 Fanning Mill, 1 wide tire Wagon, 1 Hay and Stock Rack combined, 1 spring Seat, 1 Stone Boat, 1 set Bob Sleighs, 1 Cutter, 2 set double Work Harness, 1 light Driving Harness, 1 single Harness, 1 set Leather Fly Nets, 2 Log Chains, 1 Grind Stone, 1 8-barrel Water Tank, 1 Feed Cooker, 25 Potatoe Crates, 25 Grain Bags, 2 Milk Cans, Forks, Hoes and numerous other small farm tools.

TERMS : All sums of $5.00 and under, cash. All sums over $5.00, seven months time will be given for good endorsed notes with interest at 6 per cent.

MRS. C. G. & MABEL GROVER.

J. G. SUMMERS, Auctioneer.

Hot coffee and lunch at noon.

LOOK ABOUT YOU and see the dunes that give Michigan's western shore a special flavor. Thousands find the desolation intriguing, particularly in the Sleeping Bear area where climbing up a hill of sand at Day Park is one of the things to do for youngsters—of whatever age. (AAA)

From War to Woe

WITH THE automobile industry solidly established as a major factor in Michigan's economy, there followed a period of explosive growth, and a significant shift in the pattern of population from rural to urban orientation.

War was about to break out. The great experiment in prohibition would be launched, and then would come prosperity—and the crash.

But before that date, Ford's domination of the automobile industry would have ended, the landscape of the state would be covered with housing projects, and the state would get its tallest building—the skyscraping, 56-story Penobscot in Detroit—as well as the beginning of its worst depression.

VEHICLE CITY was the boast of Flint, and a well-deserved one early in the automobile era. There, William C. Durant, with a $2,000 loan from a bank, established the Flint Road Cart Company, from which came the wherewithal and experience to make him a pioneer in the automobile business. Durant made Flint the birthplace of General Motors. He had sold a half-interest in the cart company to his friend J. Dallas Dort, owner of a hardware business, and their firm became the largest producer of carts in the country. (Journal)

AN ORIGINAL FLINT CART, which is now in the Sloan Museum in Flint. (Journal)

WILLIAM C. DURANT and J. Dallas Dort (right) stand talking near the Imperial Wheel plant in Flint in 1908. They renamed their Flint Road Cart Company the Durant-Dort Carriage Company. (Journal)

THE 1898 OFFICE of the Durant-Dort Company exuded a suitable touch of affluence. (Journal)

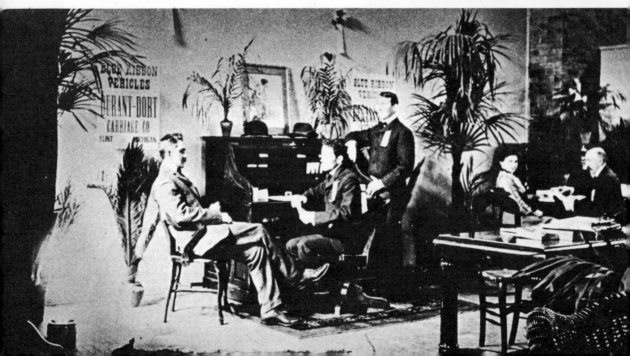

ALL SORTS OF CARS were being built in 1900, and forty-two makes were displayed at the very first automobile show that November in New York. One feature of the show was demonstration of the maneuverability of cars around an obstacle course surrounding the display area. In this scene, the driver is testing a Packard. (MVMA)

BY 1905, the auto show at the Gardens was jammed with displays and a sea of names. (MVMA)

MEANWHILE IN DETROIT, Henry Ford was trying to attract attention with a racing model at a time when automobiles were still considered sporting machines. Many years would pass before news of automobiles was off the sports pages. Auto races were attracting large crowds, however, as shown in this scene of a 1908 Savannah race won by a Fiat. Ford is shown in Detroit with a friend at the wheel of one of his first racing models. (DHM)

SEVEN DAYS BEFORE the picture above was taken, promotion-minded William C. Durant took over management of the newly moved Buick Motor Company in Flint. On November 7, 1904, the first production of the plant was lined up on Saginaw Street for all to see. Included were a couple of cars (far right) that don't seem quite finished. Interestingly enough, on the day that David Buick had decided to move his plant from Detroit to Flint, the Michigan Master Horse Shoers had wound up their Flint convention with a resolution to establish a state horseshoeing college. Flint had 14,000 people then, and a national reputation as the Vehicle City. (Journal)

AUTOMOBILE OUTINGS were a big thing as people rode around the countryside in groups, stopping off from time to time to admire the scenery. Hardy women even tried their hand at driving, with chains to help them move in the snow. (MVMA)

ROADS WERE HORRIBLE, and a lot of time was spent being pulled out of the mud as drivers engaged in all sorts of competitions to prove the roadworthiness of one car or another. One of the greatest tests came in the Glidden tours, credited by many as critical in making the car more than a sporting thing. One trophy went to the owner of a Chalmers "30" that had won a 2,851-mile contest. (MVMA)

THIS OMNIBUS, built in Pontiac by a predecessor to GM Truck, boasted of having indestructible steel wheels, although the headlamps were still the old oil-burning type. One thing about the ladies of the early 1900s—they always dressed to the teeth for whatever they were doing. (MVMA)

IT DIDN'T TAKE LONG for the automobile
to get the family into the country, and soon
a whole new industry would be spawned to
serve the needs of thousands to get away
from it all and go camping. In fact, in the
1970s the recreation vehicle became a major
factor in American automobile production.

FOR ALMOST THIRTY YEARS, these two
men, caught in a rare pose by *News* photographer Bill Kuenzel, had a major impact on
the growth and development of Michigan.
Henry Ford (left) and James Couzens started
together when the Ford Motor Company
was organized in 1903, but by 1919 Ford
had bought out Couzens and Couzens became
deeply involved in politics. He was elected
mayor of Detroit, and then United States
Senator. He and Ford were to differ again,
on a solution when Michigan's banks were
to be closed in 1933. (DHM)

EAST LANSING had all the atmosphere of the college town. Michigan State, which had been concentrating there on turning out horticulturalists and providing a quiet, idyllic library setting, was also on the verge of flexing its athletic muscle. It wouldn't be until the 1950s, however, that MSU would finally make it to the Big Ten. (MSU)

THE MICHIGAN AGGIES (now the Spartans) were scoring the first touchdown here in what proved to be their first football victory, 12 to 7, over the University of Michigan in 1913. The teams first played in 1898. Prof. R. C. Carpenter, who also taught math and civil engineering, was the MAC coach. (MSU)

A PICTURE OF SOLIDITY are these gentlemen—directors of the Dime Savings Bank—gathered for a formal meeting, probably at the Detroit Club in 1913. The Dime Bank once occupied the building now owned by Commonwealth. Henry Ford, in white tie, sits at the far left. (DHM)

Facing page, top: GREAT ACTIVITY was evident at the port of Detroit in 1910 when the Detroit and Cleveland Line provided all sorts of trips and excursions in Great Lakes waters. (Dowling)

THIS FASCINATING MAP of the D & C service area *(below)* also provides a comprehensive look at details that are rarely so well displayed. (Dowling)

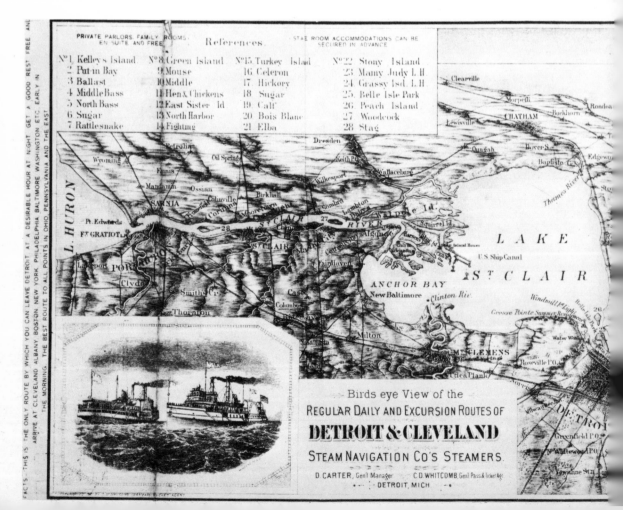

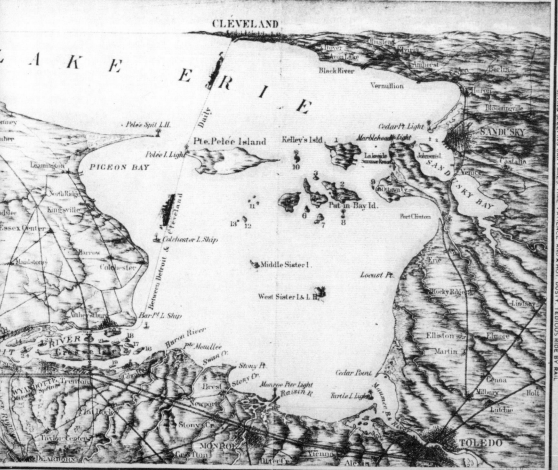

A MEMORABLE CAREER was that of Woodbridge Ferris, who started teaching school at seventeen, and fifteen years later was organizing the Big Rapids Industrial School, today's Ferris State College. Fifteen enrolled when the school opened in 1884, with Mr. and Mrs. Ferris handling most of the chores. In 1913, already established as a political leader, Ferris became the first Democrat to be governor since the mid- 1800s, and was re-elected. In 1922, he was elected as the first Democratic senator from Michigan in seventy years. He is shown above with his wife and, in an unusual picture *(below)* on the top steps of the state Capitol, taking the oath of office with other members of the ticket. (Ferris)

SALT, IT TURNED OUT, was another
major product to be found in Michigan
where a great field of it seems to run through
the Saginaw Valley to Detroit. First mined
in Saginaw in the mid-1800s, activity was
moved to Detroit when the first shaft was
sunk there in 1906, and eventually it
was being dug out by steam shovel. Another
major source developed around St. Clair, and
in Midland, the Dow Chemical Company
became one of the world's greatest chemical
producers by utilizing brine derivatives.
(DHM)

AS THEY HAVE for many years, the Daughters of the American Revolution gathered in Washington on this April day in 1917, These ladies formed the Michigan contingent to the convention. (Grand Rapids)

[150]

A LITTLE KNOWN FACET of the history of the Ford Motor Company, which gave the world the $5-day and the assembly line, was Ford's personal insistence on having enthusiastic, patriotic, thrifty workers, who also kept clean homes. He tried to achieve this by sponsoring classes in English, of which the first is shown (below), staging all sorts of pageants and ceremonies. His sociological department also sponsored a co-op which did a bit of advertising of its own to promote business. Some indication of prices about 1920 is given by the listings in the ad. (Ford)

SUDDENLY IN THE 1910s, Michigan's cities began to explode as the auto industry and World War I began to make their impact felt, and the pendulum swung quickly from rural to urban. Only 35 percent of the people lived in towns or cities of 2,500 or less in 1890. By 1920, the ratio was reversed with 61 percent living in the cities, and only 29 percent in villages and farms. Not surprisingly, of course, the major growth occurred where the auto industry was moving in.

EVEN TARPAPER SHACKS were used by people coming to Flint to live and work at the Buick plant, seen here in the background. Barely discernable at the right are houses in the process of being built. (Journal)

SUBURBAN GROWTH is dramatically demonstrated in these pictures of how Park Avenue between Nowlin and Military in Dearborn was converted from a field to a residential area in 1919. (Ford) in 1919. (Ford)

[EXTRA] # THE EVENING NEWS [EXTRA]

BATTLE CREEK, MICHIGAN

VOLUME VI. NUMBER 30. MONDAY, JUNE 11, 1917 PRICE, TWO CENTS

BATTLE CREEK GETS ARMY CAMP SITE HERE APPROVED BY WAR DEP'T.

General Barry's Recommendation Confirmed---Means Battle Creek Will Receive Camp If Suitable Site Is Made Available

Associated Press Message Received Here This Morning Tells of Approval of Site Here, and at Little Rock, Louisville and San Antonio

BULLETIN

By ASSOCIATED PRESS

WASHINGTON, June 11--Battle Creek, Mich., Little Rock, Louisville, Ky., and San Antonio, Texas, have been approved by the War Department as additional camp sites for the new army.

The question now to be settled is that of securing a site. The decision in Battle Creek's Favor means that this city will be given the opportunity to round up one of several sites at the right terms If this can ce done, Battle Creek, being first choice, will get the cantonment.

The establishment of a cantonment, as Battle Creek has already been told, means the building of a city of not less than 30,000 men.

It will house 28,000 soldiers, together with their officers. It will include 12,000 animals.

Into its construction will go not less than 4,000 carloads of materials.

The city will be composed of frame houses, but it will be complete as to sewer arrangements, electric lighting, roadways, and so forth.

A cantonment is to embrace approximately 800 acres. The government leases for one year with the privilege of three, and with a condition as to purchase.

Instructions have been given to rush work on cantonments previously located, as rapidly as possible, so that the men may be in them and under training by Sept. 1.

Making a city to house 30,000 men between now and September 1 is quite a job.

Battle Creek has three sites in prospect—one down the river covering considerably territory to the west and south, in the general neighborhood of Augusta and Harmonia; one up the Battle creek and between that stream and the Grand Trunk tracks. The property in this tract is understood to be already assembled and ready to offer.

Another site lies in the direction of Beadle lake, where it is understood, a considerable acreage is available with little if any rent.

Wherever the site is located, it will have railroad connections, probably interurban connections, telephone and telegraph, postal station, express station, and so forth.

In all particulars, it will be a city in itself.

There will be separate barracks for each company, with mess kitchen and mess hall attached.

A message to the Enquirer Saturday night announced that the secretary of war's absence from Washington had delayed action on the cantonment matter, in the selection of the Michigan-Wisconsin site.

This site is to be used as the training headquarters for the troops drawn under the draft from Michigan and Wisconsin. It is to be one of the 16 major cantonments in the United States. It has been stated that the cantonment pay-roll will run about $1,000,000 a month.

Postmaster Edward Austin, S. J. Rathbun and L. R. Greusel compose a committee representing the Chamber of Commerce which has been in Washington investigating the matter, to see just what terms of lease the government desires.

MUST INCREASE WORKERS AGAINST TUBERCULOSIS

Pittsburgh, Pa., June 11—After Susan superintendent of the Tuberculosis League of Pittsburgh, declared to an address before the National conference of charities and correction today that the United States we have an increased force at huge fee for tuberculosis nursing during the war and for some years afterward.

The present war crisis will greatly increase the problem of tuberculosis and doubtless complicate it, she said. "With the certainty that the Red Cross and the army will draw in ever-greater upon the present corps of trained nurses we are forced to give earnest, constructive consideration to the question of how to best meet this need and supplement the ranks of the workers."

Few tuberculosis nursing work as believe this need can be maintained met by nurses' aids or trained attendants. Tuberculosis hospitals provide an ideal place for just such training as these attendants should have. Further valuable assistance in tuberculosis work can be rendered by the volunteer lay workers."

This is a Bird's Eye View of the Type of Camp the Government Will Build Here. Work Starts Immediately After Site is Under Lease

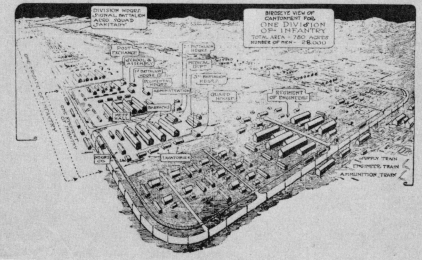

WHEN WAR WAS DECLARED, Michigan as usual provided men and a lot of the materiel. Fort Custer near Battle Creek became a gigantic training center, a boost so great for the city that the *Battle Creek News* let people know with an extra. War was declared on April 6, 1917, and the 8,000-acre Custer Complex was handling thousands of men by September. Tragically, the flu epidemic that winter sent 10,000 to the hospital, of whom 647 died. Michigan itself had 135,485 people in service, notably the distinguished Red Arrow Division. (Enquirer)

THE FIRST ARRIVALS at Fort Custer gathered in groups, waiting for instructions. (State)

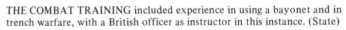

THE COMBAT TRAINING included experience in using a bayonet and in trench warfare, with a British officer as instructor in this instance. (State)

THERE WAS TIME for cards while members of an engineering corps were getting used to their equipment and the wearing of gas masks, and dancing was a part of the recreation program. (State-Willard)

ANXIETY WAS ETCHED ON THE FACES of those saying goodbye to Johnny Doughboy as he headed for war in 1917, in this case from the Michigan Central depot in Detroit. (DHM)

[156]

BUT THE SMILES and the horns came out again on the day of the Armistice in 1918, when it became apparent that the boys would be coming home again—and soon. (DHM)

SOME DOCTORS MARCHED in an Armistice Day parade. Emphasizing their feelings about America's success against the Kaiser, they carried what one writer described as "a skeleton as genuine as their smiles." (DHM)

STRINGENT FUEL RATIONING was ordered during World War I. On the first gasless Sunday, September 1, 1918, a Battle Creek policeman emphasized the news by taking time to read the paper in the middle of Capital and Michigan Avenue, then known as Jefferson and Main. (Enquirer)

All the news of all the industry while it is still news!

Of, By and For the Entire Automotive Industry.

Automotive Daily News

PASSENGER · TRUCK · TIRES · TRACTOR · ACCESSORIES

ol. 1. No. 1. NEW YORK, THURSDAY, AUGUST 27, 1925 5 Cents, $12 Per Year

Price-Cutting War in Gasoline Spreads

EW FORD CARS 'OMBINE 'EYE' AND SERVICE APPEAL

losed Bodies Seen in Colors for First Time

ecial from A. D. N. Detroit Bureau)

Detroit, Aug. 26.—Body changes, ore pronounced than any made ice the adoption of the model chassis, and numerous changes the chassis itself, were anunced here today by the Ford otor Company, with prices reaining unchanged.

Outstanding features of the anges, common to both open and losed types, are lower, all-steel dies on a lowered chassis, comte new design in most body oes larger, lower fenders, newly signed seats and larger and more werful brakes.

losed bodies, for the first time Ford history, are available in lors.

Longer lines, secured by raising e radiator and redesigning cowls d bodies, are noticeable. All cars e lower from roof to road. Wide own fenders, hung close to the heels, contribute to the general fect of lowness and smartness. ear fenders are attached direct to e body.

Nickeled Radiators

Runabout and touring cars are ll furnished in the standard ack only, but closed bodies are ished in color, with nickeled diators. Coupe and Tudor bodies me in a deep channel green, hile the Fordor's color is a rich indsor maroon.

Larger compartments, more eply cushioned seats and more room provide greater comfort driver and passenger in all odels.

Numerous conveniences and improvements have been incorporated the new cars. In the runabout, uring car, coupe and Tudor sedan, soline tank capacity has been creased from about 9½ gallons slightly over 10 gallons and the nk is suspended under the cowl parated from the engine by the sh board. It is filled through an geniously designed filler cap, cometely hidden by a cover similar appearance to a cowl ventilator. One-piece windshields and narowed roof pillars on the coupe and dor sedan produce greatly increased range of vision for the iver, and improved ventilation. y tilting the windshield downrd slightly, the front compartent is flooded with air downrd through the cowl. An ineased angle delivers direct venation to passengers.

Additional Comfort

Additional driving comfort has en secured by lowering the seats the runabout, touring car, coupe d Tudor types 2½ inches. Seats e more deeply cushioned than retofore. The steering column s been lowered three inchs in types just named, and the ering wheel increased from 16

New Ford Angle

Henry Ford has just been eulogized from the a new angle. This time it is in connection with his interest in the advancement of aviation. J. Gainor, president of the National Association of Letter Carriers, in Detroit a few weeks ago, said: "Thanks to Mr. Ford's patriotism, America will be in the front rank of preparedness in event of another war."

EUROPE SPEEDS TIRE PRODUCTION

Demand Also Grows for American-Made Brands

(Special Dispatch to Automotive Daily News)

Washington, D. C., Aug. 26.—Growing demand for American-made tires in many foreign countries and an increase in the foreign output are shown in cabled reports of tire production made public today by P. L. Palmerton, chief of the rubber division of the Department of Commerce.

Although Czecho-Slovakia offers a relatively small market for automobile tires, owing to import restrictions on motor cars, there is a noticeable upward trend in demand because of the increased domestic automotive production. As there are practically no tires manufactured in the country—the production of "Cordial" tires being unimportant—Czecho-Slovakia offers a good field for foreign makes.

American tires, particularly the well-advertised brands, are in good demand and are used in standard equipment by some manufacturers.

Order of Popularity

Foreign tires, other than American, solf in Czecho-Slovakia, are as follows, in the order of their popularity: Michelin, Continental, Austrian Semperit, Dunlop and Italian Pirelli.

German tire exports in May reached the highest figure for any month this year, numbering 22,062

PENN CO. ASKS FULL PROBE OF ITS ACTIVITIES

Oil Substitution Suit Called Standard Suit To Hit Competition

Washington, Aug. 27.—(By A. D. N. Service).—"The suit filed against the Penn Oil Company in connection with the alleged misuse of the name "Mobiloil" is another attempt of the Standard Oil interests to discredit competition in the oil industry." Alvin L. Newmyer, attorney for the Penn Oil Company, declared in a statement made public today.

The bill in equity against the Penn Oil Company was filed on behalf of the Vacuum Oil Company of New York, by the National Better Business Bureau, as part of a national campaign to stamp out the oil substitution evil.

Mr. Newmyer declared the Penn Oil Company does not offer for sale "mobiloil," or any other product of the Standard Oil Company, of which the Vacuum Oil Company is a subsidiary. "We would welcome," said Mr. Newmyer, "a complete and impartial investigation by the Better Business Bureau and we are confident that the accusation will not only be conclusively disproved, but the real motive behind the action exposed."

VACUUM CO. ANSWER

New York, Aug. 27.—"Here is our answer to the Penn Oil Company," said F. W. Lovejoy, director of sales promotion for the Vacuum Oil Company, to the Automotive Daily News, as he pointed to a letter from the National Better Business Bureau. The letter contained an announcement as follows:—

"The statement of the attorneys for the Penn Oil Company to the effect that the company would welcome a Better Business Bureau investigation of the charges that it has been substituting inferior for high grade oils, has been brought to our attention. The best answer that we can make is that the investigation upon which the Vacuum Oil Company makes its application for an injunction against the Penn Oil Company was conducted under the National Better Business Bureau direction and evidence to be introduced at the hearing before Supreme Court Justice McAvoy was collected by our own investigators."

In the suit against the Peen Oil Company it is alleged that oil being sold as "Mobiloil A" was actually crankcase drainings, which had been imperfectly reclaimed. Numerous cases were found, according to the investigator, where motorists were paying $1.20 a gallon for what they thought was high grade oil.

GOOD GLASS DEMAND

Demand for plate glass continues good in Pittsburgh, and distributors appear to be satisfied with present prices.

S. D. PLANS FOR WINTER

It is announced that South Da-

Over-Production Blamed For Drastic Reductions

New York, Aug. 27.—Further drastic reductions in the price of gasoline were forecast today as the important companies in the industry gave indications of continuing the spectacular price-cutting which has been in progress for some time. The Tide Water Oil Company left its competitors gasping when it announced a 3-cent reduction in tank-wagon prices yesterday, but the Gulf Refining Company and the Standard of New York promptly met the drop. Other companies were preparing today to do likewise.

Under the new schedule of prices Tide Water is quoting gasoline at 17 cents a gallon, tank wagon, in greater New York, Staten Island, 3 cents below the price quoted Yonkers and Long Island. This is yesterday by Standard Oil of New York. The Standard of New Jersey has lowered its tank wagon price ½ cent a gallon throughout its territory, making the new price 16 cents. This reduction was immediately met by the Tide Water, Gulf Refining, Sinclair Consolidated and Texas Company.

In the New England states the Atlantic Refining reduced gasoline prices 2 cents a gallon and this reduction was met today by the Standard of New York, Gulf Oil, Texas and other competing companies. The Atlantic Refining also announced a cut of 1 cent, to take effect today in Pennsylvania and Delaware.

While the reductions have revived talk of a trade war, the executives of the leading marketing companies refuse to admit that any such conflict is under way. The origin of the present situation, they point out, is plain enough to those who have been watching the production figures. There has been a marked overproduction of gasoline in recent months. The producing companies, misled by the optimistic talk about probable demand, some months ago began to employ the cracking process with such vigor that they soon found themselves in possession of growing stocks in the face of a demand which, while large, was below expectations.

Further Drop Foreseen

Washington, Aug. 27.—Gasoline prices in Washington will drop this year to 1924's 16 cent level and probably lower, Paul Himmelfarb, Penn Oil Company president, predicted today.

Gasoline dropped one half a cent a gallon in Washington today, the fourth price cut in seventeen days. This is the biggest series of drops in local gasoline selling history, Himmelfarb said.

Today's reduction brings the service station price here to 21 cents and the tank wagon price to 18 cents. The cut follows two 1 cent and one ½ cent reductions since August 8.

Overproduction of crude oil in California and a dull export market is responsible for the price descent, Himmelfarb explained. California is producing 5,000,000 gallons of gasoline daily, he said, and 3,000,000 gallons of this floods the Eastern market. With little gasoline being exported, the Pennsylvania producers have been forced to cut prices to withstand the

Moon Reduces Prices On Cars $50 to $250

Chicago, Aug. 26.—The Moon Motor Car Company has announced price reductions of $50 on the touring car and $250 on the sedan.

RALPH B. DORT CONTESTS WILL

Flint, Mich., Aug. 27.—Ralph Bates Dort, eldest son of the late J. Dallas Dort and one time advertising manager and foreign representative of the Dort Motor Car Company, has appealed his father's will, which was recently admitted to probate here.

Ralph charges it isn't his father's last will; it doesn't express the true intention of the testator; that his father was unduly influenced, and that it does not provide for lawful disposition of property.

Dated July 13, 1916, the will leaves the estate to the widow and three other children. Only mention of Ralph was: "I am not unmindful that I have another son, Ralph Bates Dort, who is not named in this will, but his name is intentionally omitted for reasons which I deem sufficient."

The father settled a large trust fund on Ralph several years ago when he had a guardian appointed for him. Since Mr. Dort's death in May the son has succeeded in having the guardianship removed.

Exports $60,000,000 Autos to Tropics

New York, Aug. 24.—Exports of $60,000,000 worth of American automobiles to the tropics in the fiscal year just ended, coupled with the fact that practically all our airplanes and one-half of our wireless apparatus exported go to that section, suggests, says the Trade Record of the National City Bank, that the people of the tropical world are finding in these new devices a partial solution of their transportation problem. The tropical and subtropical belt, which stretches around the globe between the 30th parallel of north latitude and the 30th parallel of south latitude, has about 600,000,000 people.

CHEVROLET AT PEAK OUTPUT

Plants of the Chevrolet Motor Company are operating day and

SPEAKING OF GASOLINE, here's the front page of the first issue of the *Automotive Daily News,* which later was shifted to Detroit and became a weekly. Note the headlines.

A SEVERE WINTER came in 1917-1918 that was climaxed by the start of the great influenza epidemic which killed thousands in Michigan and, according to some historians, about 25 million people worldwide. The first Michigan case was reported in March 1918, and the disease didn't run its course until early 1919. (Willard)

TWO MEN DOMINATED the state's political life during the 1920s—Alexander J. Groesbeck, who was governor from 1920 to 1926, and Fred Green, who served from 1927 through 1930. The Groesbeck family were pioneers in Warren Township, and Alex first tasted politics when his father was elected Macomb County sheriff. He studied law at the University of Michigan, served as attorney general for two terms from 1916 to 1920, and earned the reputation there of streamlining the government while head of the state. Green, reputed to have more personal friends than any man in Michigan, defeated Groesbeck in the 1926 primary after a bitter battle. He, too, was progressive in highway building and conservation, established the first statewide police radio system, and appointed Arthur Vandenberg to the Senate on the death of Woodbridge Ferris. Green is shown during a golf game at Mackinac Island about 1927. (Free Press-State)

MICHIGAN WAS AMONG the first to establish a Board of Health in 1873. In the 1920s, its public health nurses were involved in scores of educational activities. In the picture above, a group of them sits on the lawn for an official session. (State)

THE BEST SUBSTITUTE

If you cannot nurse your baby
Give him fresh, clean milk from
healthy cows
BUT
Cow's milk was meant for calves

To fit it for your baby
IT MUST BE MODIFIED
Don't Ask Your Neighbors
Don't Ask Your Relatives
ASK THE DOCTOR

ALL SORTS OF SIGNS and brochures were prepared to drive home the need for public health awareness. This one is a bit anti-quated now in view of further developments in public health.

EXAMINATIONS IN SCHOOLS were made regularly to check eyes, ears, throat, height, and weight. This scene is at a consoli-dated school near Lansing in the 1920s. (State)

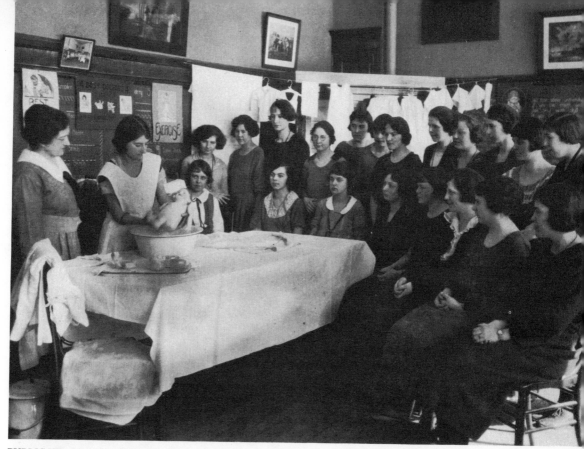

PUBLIC HEALTH NURSES took time to teach classes of the "Little Mother's League" in high school. They also made calls to assist mothers at their homes, which sometimes had the mixed quality of beauty and despair that the photographer has caught in the photo below. (State)

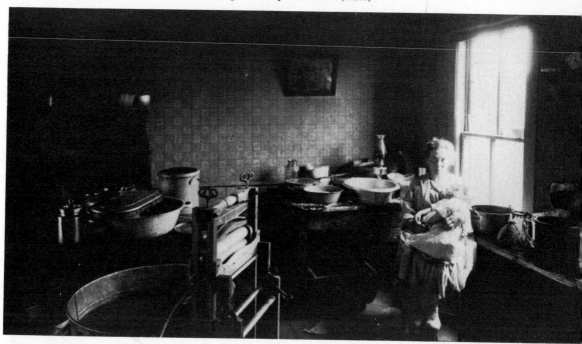

INTEGRATION? Well, Frank Seymour, many years later a successful public affairs counselor, said it was achieved in "our gang" in the early 1920s in a northwest Detroit neighborhood. "But then the pressure forced dad to move his family," he admitted ruefully. Seymour's father was a steam engineer at the Ford plant. "He helped to build the Rouge plant," said Frank. The Seymours are shown with their Ford in their Warrington Avenue (then Crudder) backyard, and Frank is in front with a big smile in the group picture that includes his brother and sister and neighbors. "We're still in touch," said Seymour.

[162]

SOMETHING NEW attracted attention in Battle Creek in 1923 when a street signal, controlled by a policeman from a station at the side of the street, made its appearance. It was one of many ways devised over the years for traffic control. (Enquirer)

A RARE PHOTO INDEED is this one of Tyrus (Ty) Cobb, usually seen sliding with spikes flying or grimly swinging a bat. A master at both skills, Cobb started his first game with the Detroit Tigers on August 20, 1905, and helped Detroit to win pennants in 1907-08-09. He posted an almost unbelievable .369 lifetime batting average in his twenty years with the team. He had 200 or more hits in nine seasons, and stole as many as 96 bases in 1915, his best year. (DHM)

ELABORATE IS THE WORD to describe the decorations for this Michigan State J-Hop of 1922, but then, J-Hops were the big things in college life in those days. So why not form MAC (it was Michigan Agricultural College then) as part of the Grand March of the evening? (MSU)

ON JULY 4, 1924, Henry Ford decided to show off his collection of old cars, which served as a nucleus for his great Ford Museum. So they staged a parade in Dearborn, and Ford provided an extra touch by showing up in top hat and mutton chops to drive a carriage. His wife and grandchildren, Henry Ford II and Benson, shared the trip. Later he posed solo with his namesake. (Ford)

[164]

LIKE OTHER AMERICANS, many in Michigan came disillusioned out of World War I, into which they had gone as sort of a crusade, and with a hatred that had been stimulated by anti-German feelings during the war. In this setting, the Ku Klux Klan revived its message of 100-percent Americanism and rumors and negative feelings about Jews, Catholics, blacks, and foreigners. It built up considerable strength for a time as this July 4, 1925, gathering in Grand Rapids suggests. (Wayne)

WITH PROHIBITION, another major factor for change arrived. Michigan, true to its Yankee heritage, had agitated for prohibition for years, and became dry on May 1, 1918, more than a year before the 18th Amendment took effect. It had passed its first prohibition law in 1855, but the legislature had backtracked, permitting manufacture and sale of wine and beer not to be drunk on the premises. In 1875 that act was repealed. In 1887, a local option law was passed, and in 1916 state voters endorsed another prohibition law, but those who thought this a great victory soon learned of the evils that prohibition could bring. The picture above shows bootleggers heading for their cars with suitcases full of liquor they have gotten from a boat just over from Canada. The photograph was taken by Monroe Stroecker of the *Detroit News*.

[165]

FORTY-SIX GUESTS of the 588 who gathered to celebrate Ann Arbor's one hundredth birthday in 1925, all of them descendants of the early pioneers: In the background may be seen "Ann's Arbor," which was conspicuous in the decorations of the University of Michigan Union banquet hall. The wives of Ann Arbor's founders were named Ann. (Burton)

WILL ROGERS in Henry Ford's one-seat flivver airplane: Ford, who succeeded pretty much in his goal to put everyone on wheels, also thought he might get everyone in the air in this plane that would be "safe, inexpensive and reliable." Harry Brooks piloted the first one on July 30, 1926, and took to commuting to his Birmingham home in it, amazing the neighbors as he landed on small vacant fields, roadways, and sidewalks. It could travel 85 miles an hour, and was far advanced in much of its design. Charles Lindbergh flew it in 1927. Ford lost interest after Brooks crashed into the Atlantic near Melbourne, Florida, and was killed, but not before setting a record of 1,000 miles on 50 gallons of gas. (Ford)

LINDY'S MOTHER, Mrs. Evangeline Land Lindbergh, was a teacher at Detroit's Cass Tech in 1927 when Charles Lindbergh flew the Atlantic. John Lodge, then acting mayor and president of the Common Council and also her uncle, greeted Mrs. Lindbergh (left) at City Hall after the good news that her son had landed in Paris. With them were Mrs. Edwin Lodge (second from right) and Lodge's wife Harriett. (DHM)

GENERAL MOTORS was experimenting with a small car while Ford was trying to produce flying flivvers. This 1925 car was designed by Fabio Segardi (at the wheel) for the General Motors research staff. It was never put into production—but look at the small cars today! (GM)

THE PROVERBIAL SENIORS' TRIP was taken by this serious-looking group of Hamtramck High students in 1925. As was the custom of the time, they wound up in Washington, D. C., and made the ritual trip to Mt. Vernon. (HPL)

A SHOCKING EVENT in Michigan history occurred in Bath in May 1927, when the town's consolidated school was dynamited and thirty-eight children and seven adults were killed. The incident was triggered by Andrew Kehoe, a farmer who sought revenge because of increased taxes he had to pay to build the school. Firemen and other rescuers rushed to the scene and then set up a morgue on the school grounds. Sen. James Couzens contributed the money to build another school, and Prof. C. E. Angell of the University of Michigan created the statue of a child that was placed in the foyer. (Free Press-State)

FOUNDER JOSEPH MADDY pauses from conducting the first Interlochen orchestra in 1928 in a bowl built by borrowing $15,000 to start construction of forty camp buildings. Maddy was given fifty acres on Green Lake by William Pennington in exchange for a boarding contract at his hotel. In the 1930s, the camp bought out the Hotel Pennington.

THE GREAT PAUL WHITEMAN came to camp in 1941 to play in a benefit concert, as have many other stars. As happens too, he took time to work with youngsters. The camp attracts musicians, age eight through college years, from all over the world. Recently a year-round academy of the arts has been started at Interlochen.

WITH A BACKDROP of Green Lake, students of the harp create a pleasant picture.

GRAND RAPIDS' own Arthur Vandenberg, destined to become a leader in the United States Senate, had just been appointed to fill the vacancy caused by the death of Sen. Woodbridge Ferris. Moments before this picture, he had paid his respects to Pres. Calvin Coolidge, then stepped outside to pose on the White House steps with Barbara, Mrs. Vanderberg, Betty, and Arthur, Jr. The date was April 8, 1928. (Free Press)

THERE'S NOTHING LIKE a wedding. The Henry Rummels of Frankenmuth were blessed with a great turnout for theirs around 1925, and just about everyone got into the picture. (Frankenmuth)

Volume VIII.   L   Dearborn, Mich., December 15, 1927   Number 4

TEN PER CENT OF U. S. POPULATION SEES NEW FORD FIRST DAY OF SHOW

New Iron Mine Is Fine Plant

Surface Structure Is Standard Ford Building

Named by Henry Ford, Planned and Constructed for Maximum of Safety and Efficiency

The new iron mine of the Ford Motor Company owes its name to Henry Ford. Mr. Ford visited the property on his trip to the Upper Peninsula in 1926. The mine lies in a rich blueberry-producing district, and at the time of Mr. Ford's visit the crop was at its peak. As Mr. Ford gathered a handful of the berries near the site of the present shaft, he remarked: "I have a name for this mine; we will call it the 'Blueberry'." And the Blueberry it has been called ever since.

That was in the fall. The work of clearing the ground for the shaft and buildings had begun only in September. Today, fifteen months later, the surface plant stands practically com-

Concluded on page 6

3,281-Mile Trip in Ninety Hours New Car Record

Leaving Dearborn at 10:05 a. m. December 2 in a new Model A Ford car, Ray Dahlinger, manager of Henry Ford Farms at Dearborn, arrived in Los Angeles, California, at 1:02 a. m., Tuesday, December 6, completing the run in 89 hours and 57 minutes. This constitutes the longest cross-country run made by one of the new cars up to the present time, proving its ability to stand up under trying conditions. No difficulty was experienced en route, although the car was driven at high speed most of the way.

The car used by Mr. Dahlinger was a standard stock model Tudor sedan taken directly from the assembly line at Fordson. No additional testing or inspection was given it other than that which all cars receive during their construction.

Henry Ford accompanied Mr. Dahlinger for the first thirty-three miles, to Saline, Michigan.

Schedule of prices new CAR and TRUCK	
Phaeton	$395
Roadster	385
Sedan—Two Door	495
Sedan—Four Door	570
Coupe	495
Sport Coupe	550
Chassis	325
AA Truck chassis	460
Express Body and Cab	140
Platform Body and Cab	135
Stake Body and Cab	150

All Prices F.O.B. Detroit.

Eager Crowds Block Traffic in Effort to Gain First Look at New Model; Newspapers Feature Event

Rain, Sleet, Snow and Sub-Zero Temperatures Fail to Dampen Enthusiasm of Millions; Record Unequaled in History

Tremendous enthusiasm marked the first day's showing, on December 2, of the new Model A Ford car throughout the United States, Canada, and foreign countries. Traffic was blocked in many cities by the crowds. Wherever people met, it was the chief topic of discussion. It was featured on the front page of all leading newspapers, and in Dallas, Texas, extra editions proclaimed the event the "greatest since the signing of the Armistice."

An accurate check of the first day's attendance at all places where the car was displayed and at dealers' establishments throughout the United States gave a total of 10,534,992, or nearly 10 per cent of the total population of the country. The crowds on the following days nearly equaled those of the first, making a total which included approximately one-quarter of the country's population. In Pittsburgh, 12½ per cent of the city's population saw the car during the first day.

Despite torrents of rain in the South and the East, snow and driving sleet farther north, and below-zero temperatures in the north-central section, the attendance everywhere surpassed all expectations. At most display points extra police were required to keep traffic moving.

At Convention Hall in Detroit, where forty cars were on display, 114,849 people visited the exhibit during the first day's showing. Seventy-five policemen were necessary to handle the crowds and prevent traffic jams.

Within a few minutes after the doors were opened, spectators were grouped eight and ten deep around all the exhibits, and by the end of the first hour it was difficult to approach any of them.

The new models were also on display at the sales showroom at the Highland Park plant, 31,368 people visiting this exhibition the first day.

In Milwaukee, Wisconsin, a hastily constructed fence was necessary to prevent the packed masses of humanity from breaking the showroom windows. In Los Angeles, California, a crowd began to assemble at 7 a. m. and grew until it blocked traffic.

Concluded on page 8

J. W. Capek, manager Los Angeles branch, Ford Motor Company, congratulating Mr. Dahlinger upon his arrival in Los Angeles with the first transcontinental Model A Ford. At right, Arthur H. Vultee, sales manager for Hamlin W. Nerney, Inc., Los Angeles Ford dealer and Duke Kahanamoku, Hawaiian Olympic and world champion swimmer.

IT WAS RATHER PHENOMENAL—the introduction of the Model A in 1927. Consider that radio was an infant and there was no television; yet one out of every ten Americans went to a showroom on December 2, 1927, to get a look at a new car. There was a reason. As the leader for years, having produced fifteen million Model Ts, Ford in 1927 found itself losing ground. Suddenly, the company shut down—completely, with thousands laid off for several months and Detroit hurt. Then came word that THE car was ready. Detroit's Convention Hall *(above)* was the scene for one showing; the Chicago Armory *(below)* was hardly able to hold the throng gathered there. (Ford-Sorenson)

WEATHER
Cloudy Tonight and Frizss

THE MUSKEGON CHRONICLE EXTRA

VOL. LI—NO. 120. MUSKEGON, MICHIGAN, THURSDAY, OCTOBER 24, 1929 TWENTY-TWO PAGES. THREE CENTS.

BODIES FROM 'MILWAUKEE' ARE PICKED UP OFF RACINE

Ill-Fated Grand Trunk Carferry, Milwaukee

Above is a picture of the ill-fated Grand Trunk carferry, Milwaukee, lost in the storm that raged over Lake Michigan for the last three days. Bodies and wreckage from the ship have been found and no hope is held out for the lives of any of her crew of 52 persons.

GRAND TRUNK CARFERRY AND CREW OF 52 MEN GO DOWN IN STORM ON LAKE MICHIGAN

The Grand Trunk carferry, Milwaukee, and her crew of 52 men, are lost.

The ship went down in the terrific gale at about 9:30 p. m. Tuesday as she was fighting her way across Lake Michigan to Grand Haven after leaving Milwaukee at 2:30 the same afternoon.

The last faint hope that the ship might be safe and seeking shelter in some out of the way spot came this afternoon when several bodies and wreckage were found off the Wisconsin shore near Racine and Kenosha.

Capt. Robert McKay and more than 39 of the officers and members of the crew came from Grand Haven. Members of the families and other relatives of the men gathered at the Grand Trunk offices there pleading for news that the ship was safe. Then came the news that the bodies bearing life preservers from the Milwaukee had been found.

Grief stricken relatives, wives, mothers and children returned to their homes to be alone in their deep sorrow.

The first information that the ship had foundered came in a wireless message Capt. Dipert of the Ludington coast guard station intercepted. This message said that a lifeboat had been found off Wisconsin.

Then came the news from Milwaukee that Capt. Ray Howard of the steamer Colonel

(Continued on Page 2)

MILLIONS LOSS IN STORM

DEBRIS STREWS GREAT LAKES AS GALE SUBSIDES

Ship Missing, One Sunken, Four Aground During Blow

FORD BARGE CREW SAFE

Chicago Damage to Exceed $3,000,000; Michigan Hard Hit

By THE ASSOCIATED PRESS

The howling winds which have swept peril across the Great Lakes since last Sunday subsided somewhat today leaving one vessel missing, another at the bottom of Lake Erie, four grounded. Wreckage was strewn along hundreds of miles of waterfront indicating a property loss which may run into the millions.

...

CITY OF MUSKEGON SANK 10 YEARS AGO

...

COAST GUARD CREW FEARED LOST ARE SAFE

...

Stocks Break In Panic

McKay Made Master Of Milwaukee Two Years Ago

Had Sailed Great Lakes for 50 Years; Wife Has Hopes Her Husband Will Be Picked Up Alive.

Grand Haven, Oct. 24.—Robert M McKay, 113 Franklin street, Grand Haven, was made master of the Grand Trunk carferry Milwaukee two years ago after 50 years of sailing on the Great Lakes.

...

Milwaukee Captain Intended to Retire At End of Year

Captain Robert McKay of the Grand Trunk carferry, Milwaukee, master of the ill-fated vessel...

Grand Trunk Office At Grand Haven Is Scene of Mourning

The Grand Trunk office at Grand Haven was a scene of mourning and sobs this afternoon.

...

SECOND MATE NOT ABOARD MILWAUKEE

...

HOOVER TRAIN NEARLY VICTIM OF AUTO PLOT

3 Men Push Car Off Tracks as Special Thunders By

TWO NEGROES NABBED

Admit Leaving Automobile on Crossing to Collect Insurance

(The text of President Hoover's address to Louisville can be found on Page 13.)

New Albany, Ind., Oct. 24.—P—An alleged plot which would have brought death to President Hoover as his train...

BILLIONS LOST IN 10 MILLION SHARE TRADING

Bankers' Meet at J. P. Morgan Offices Revives Confidence

ALL RECORDS BROKEN

Ticker Two Hours Behind Market at Two O'Clock

New York, Oct. 24.—(AP)—A stock market panic appeared to have been checked early this afternoon on a leading bankers issued reassurances and prices of some leading stocks, after declining $10 to $40 a share, rebounded sharply. At two o'clock the ticker was two hours behind the market.

...

Kidnaped Detroit Boy, 5, Returned To Home; 4 Held

Father Paid $25,000 for Release, Police Assert; Child Tells of Spending Some Time on Farm.

Detroit, Oct. 24.—Jackie Thompson, five, who was kidnaped from in front of his home September 20, was returned unharmed to his parents last night and Henry O Thompson, his father...

BROTHER OF NURSE HERE PURSER ON MILWAUKEE

...

MISSOURI, ALABAMA ARE BACK ON RUNS

...

GRAND HAVEN STUNNED BY NEW LAKE TRAGEDY

By GERALD B. DORREN
Chronicle Staff Writer

Grand Haven, Oct. 24.—Western Michigan in general and Grand Haven in particular today staggered under the news that it is the center of a third lake tragedy. Wreckage discovered along the Wisconsin shore has proven to be a victim of another disaster along this shore of Lake Michigan.

The blackest of the eyes of the big freighter, including Capt. Robert McKay, master of the ship, are believed to have gone into port in their home city.

Many of the others came from homes in both the east and west shore and the lake which claimed their lives.

Relatives Seek News

Phones of the Grand Trunk freight office and the United States coast guard service here on Wind street...

...

(Continued on Page 2)

A DAY OF DISASTER could well be the title for this front page of the *Muskegon Chronicle* which led with the sinking of a car ferry that took fifty-two lives. Played well down on the page is the fact of the great stock market collapse. Also down on the page was the story of one of Michigan's more dramatic kidnap stories—with a happy ending.

OUT OF THIS HOLE rose the first part of what was to be the tallest building in Michigan, the Penobscot, at the corner of Fort and Griswold in Detroit. The Penobscot tower would rise fifty-six stories to the left of this section, and remain unchallenged until the 1970s when a new hotel in the Renaissance Center would rise to seventy stories. The Penobscot later became the City National Bank Building. (Penobscot)

[173]

THE TOWER WENT UP in stages and finally, when completed, the Penobscot Building provided Detroit with a new downtown image. But still adding a touch of graciousness and a tie to the past were the Hammond Building, Detroit's first ten-story skyscraper of iron and concrete, and the venerable old City Hall. They made for a happy and pleasant combination at the heart of the City.

LOOK ABOUT YOU and see the wondrous Lake of the Clouds, deep in a 58,000-acre wilderness area at the west end of the Upper Peninsula. Surrounding it are the Porcupine Mountains. (AAA)

To a Grinding Halt

HAVING TASTED PROSPERITY in the twenties, Michigan came to a grinding halt in the thirties with the Depression bringing major political and social upheavals, a bank holiday, and strikes. Yet there were times to enjoy festivals and to cheer heroes—athletic and otherwise.

Another champion of the underdog emerged on the Michigan political scene when Frank Murphy, third of three children of a closely knit Harbor Beach Irish family, was elected mayor of Detroit on the eve of the Depression, and later became governor on the day after the state's first major sitdown strike.

In 1930, in an unprecedented move, Detroit voters recalled their mayor, Charles E. Bowles, and Murphy was elected to fill the vacancy that summer. A few hours after recall results were known, Jerry Buckley, an influential radio commentator who had played a major role in the recall of Bowles, was murdered in the LaSalle Hotel lobby.

HORSEBACK RIDING was one of Murphy's
favorite sports. Murphy, who served as governor
general of the Phillipines at one time, was later also
named attorney general by Pres. Franklin Roosevelt.
He is shown here with J. Edgar Hoover in that
role. He wound up his career as a member of the
Supreme Court. (Free Press)

[176]

MICHIGAN BEGAN TO SEE bitter reaction to soaring unemployment rates when, in 1932, crowds
protested in a downtown Detroit demonstration. Rates reached forty-three percent for non-agricul-
tural workers in 1931. Communist-sympathizers triggered the tieup downtown. (Wayne)

EIGHT-DAY HOLIDAY FOR ALL BANKS IN MICHIGAN

CITY EDITION

DETROIT TIMES

Only Detroit Newspaper Carrying International News   EVENING   Universal Service and Complete Sport Dispatches

EXTRA

33D YEAR, NO. 137   DETROIT, MICHIGAN, TUESDAY, FEBRUARY 14, 1933   24 PAGES   THREE CENTS

Proclamation Closing Banks to Protect State

Whereas, in view of the acute financial emergency now existing in the city of Detroit and throughout the state of Michigan, I deem it necessary in the public interest and for the preservation of the public peace, health and safety, and for the equal safeguarding without preference of the rights of all depositors in the banks and trust companies of this state and at the request of the Michigan Bankers' Association and the Detroit Clearing House and after consultation with the banking authorities, both national and state, with representatives of the United States Treasury Department, the Banking Department of the State of Michigan, the Federal Reserve Bank, the Reconstruction Finance Corporation, and with the United States Secretary of Commerce, I hereby proclaim the days from Tuesday, February 14th, 1933, to Tuesday, February 21st, 1933, both dates inclusive, to be public holidays during which time all banks, trust companies and other financial institutions conducting a banking or trust business within the state of Michigan shall not be opened for the transaction of banking or trust business, the same to be recognized, classed and treated and have the same effect in respect to such banks, trust companies and other financial institutions as other legal holidays under the laws of this state, provided that it shall not affect the making or execution of agreements or instruments in writing or interfere with judicial proceedings. Dated this 14th day of February, 1933, 1:32 a. m.

WILLIAM A. COMSTOCK, Governor of the State of Michigan.

SCHAAF SUCCUMBS ... OPERATION

STATEMENTS BY OFFICIALS

GOVERNOR COMSTOCK   Treasury...

UNION GUARDIAN TRUST CO DIFFICULTY ...

THE BIGGEST SHOCK of all came on the morning of February 14, 1933, when Gov. William Comstock signed a decree closing all the banks in Michigan. A few days later, banks were reopened to enable people to draw no more than five percent of their savings, but crowds were not much larger than usual. By the end of the year, however, the City of Detroit had to turn to scrip to pay off employes and suppliers. All sorts of charges were made in connection with the bank closings, but finally in 1934, a grand jury marched out of its quarters to declare no cause of action against a score of prominent bank officials who had been accused. (Free Press)

[177]

IN GRAND RAPIDS, Mayor George Wilson Welsh moved quickly to set up for distribution of food and for providing jobs. Canning bees were held and centers were established for supplies, including at one time some 27,000 bushels of potatoes *(facing page, top)*. Men working at terracing along the Grand River made a picture remindful of a bygone day when everything man did had to be done by hand. (Grand Rapids)

ONE OF THE BEST WAYS the government found to combat the Depression was establishment of the Civilian Conservation Corps (CCC) camps. During the winter of 1936, about a hundred men were taken to Isle Royale where they worked isolated for several months, cutting their own wood and relying solely on large fuel and food supplies stored to carry them through. (Free Press)

WHEN THINGS SEEMED at their worst in the early 1930s, Dr. William H. Peck and his wife Fannie exhibited unusual insight by organizing two major black groups to minimize particularly the Depression's effect on black business people. Dr. Peck was pastor of Bethel AME and founder of the Booker T. Washington Association, while his wife had started a Housewives League on June 10, 1930. It was the first such organization among black women, and soon she was talking about it to groups nationwide. Eventually, a national housewives association was formed, and Mrs. Peck (fifth from left above) was named president. (Burton)

DEPRESSION OR NOT, life went on and the circus came to town, featuring Daisy, the midget who had gained notoriety by sitting on the lap of J. P. Morgan during a 1932 Congressional hearing on banking. Daisy was not averse to joining the barker to stimulate attendance at her show. (Free Press)

STARTED IN 1931, the Holland Tulip Festival has become a major highlight of the Michigan festival schedule that attracts widespread attention. While the tulips are featured of course, in a real sense the festival calls repeated attention to the city and Dutch traditions. The Rev. Albertus C. Van Raalte, his wife, five children, and fifty-three followers fled to America to avoid religious persecution. They stopped in Detroit in the winter of 1846, then went on to found the city of Holland on Lake Michigan. In 1851, they established the school that became Hope College. Each May, the city turns to a week of festivities, which include queens, a parade, and a traditional washing of the streets by whoever happens to be governor. Gov. G. Mennen Williams did the honors in 1950. (Free Press-State)

[181]

MILLIONS OF ACRES had been denuded by extensive lumbering before serious thought was given to reforestation plans. They moved slowly until 1929 when Albert Stoll, conservation editor of the *Detroit News,* triggered a drive combining private and state resources. Within weeks, several thousand acres were replanted, and momentum grew for a new greening of the state. Under Stoll's plan, $2.50 would pay for Norway, white, or jack pine seedlings to plant a 40-acre section in the state reservation, and the *News* provided markers for participants. Hundreds did participate, and the results are quite evident today for those traveling through the upper part of the Lower Peninsula and the Upper Peninsula.

REFORESTATION PLANS were designed for this sort of barren wasteland.

ONE GROUP LOOKS at the kind of seedlings they will be planting.

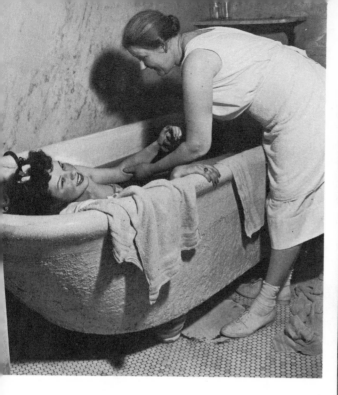

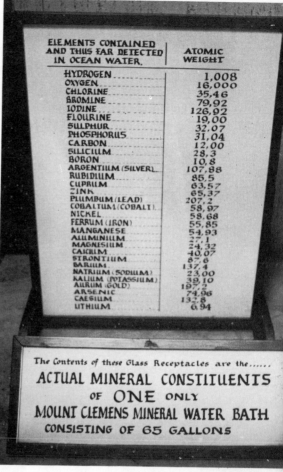

ELEMENTS CONTAINED AND THUS FAR DETECTED IN OCEAN WATER.	ATOMIC WEIGHT
HYDROGEN	1,008
OXYGEN	16,000
CHLORINE	35,46
BROMINE	79,92
IODINE	126,92
FLOURINE	19,00
SULPHUR	32,07
PHOSPHORUS	31,04
CARBON	12,00
SILICIUM	28,3
BORON	10,8
ARGENTIUM (SILVER)	107,88
RUBIDIUM	85.5
CUPRUM	63,57
ZINK	65,37
PLUMBUM (LEAD)	207,2
COBALTUM (COBALT)	58,97
NICKEL	58,68
FERRUM (IRON)	55,85
MANGANESE	54,93
ALUMINIUM	27,1
MAGNESIUM	24,32
CALCIUM	40,07
STRONTIUM	87,6
BARIUM	137,4
NATRIUM (SODIUM)	23,00
KALIUM (POTASSIUM)	39,10
AURUM (GOLD)	197,2
ARSENIC	74,96
CAESIUM	132,8
LITHIUM	6,94

The Contents of these Glass Receptacles are the......
ACTUAL MINERAL CONSTITUENTS
OF **ONE** ONLY
MOUNT CLEMENS MINERAL WATER BATH
CONSISTING OF 65 GALLONS

MINERAL BATHS helped to put Mount Clemens on the map years ago, but the era was to end in the 1960s. At the peak, more than 100,000 people from all over, including Europe, used to come to the spas and bathe in the hot mineral waters. But there was one drawback. The odor was hard to take for people who lived in the area. When they weren't bathing, people enjoyed spending time on the veranda of one of the many hotels. (Free Press)

[183]

WAYNE STATE, one building strong, sat in solitary splendor *(below)* in the heart of Detroit's residential center in 1934. By the 1970s, Wayne's campus covered most of the surrounding property, and from about a 7,000 enrollment at the time of this photo it had pushed to about 35,000. The students hadn't changed much though, from the serious approach to classes shown *(above)* by these art students in 1935. (Wayne)

THE ENTIRE STATE joined in the frenzy of the pennant drives by the Detroit Tigers in 1934 and 1935, and one of the real heroes was Lynwood (Schoolboy) Rowe. His great right arm won sixteen games in a row at one point in 1934 to tie an American League record, and helped to add the World Series to the 1935 achievements of the Tigers. But there came a time when Schoolboy called it quits, and *Detroit News* photographer Rolland Ransom captured that poignant moment when Schoolboy walked alone across the mound at Navin Field in 1938. (DHM)

BARNEY OLDFIELD, the first man to drive faster than a mile a minute, made a comeback at the 1934 World's Fair to win a Jinx-Day Derby. Old cars were used, and they averaged thirteen miles an hour for the distance. Barney, who drove a 1904 Maxwell, is shown with the usual cigar in his mouth. (MVMA)

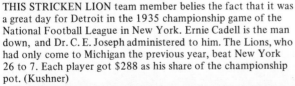

THIS STRICKEN LION team member belies the fact that it was a great day for Detroit in the 1935 championship game of the National Football League in New York. Ernie Cadell is the man down, and Dr. C. E. Joseph administered to him. The Lions, who had only come to Michigan the previous year, beat New York 26 to 7. Each player got $288 as his share of the championship pot. (Kushner)

THIS ROUTINE PICTURE of a fellow ready to center the football took on great meaning several years later when the man became president of the United States. Gerald Ford played for the University of Michigan from where he graduated in 1935. He was considered a pretty fair center by Coach Harry Kipke. (Free Press)

FEW PEOPLE made as big an impact in Michigan in the 1930s as Joe Louis, the kid from the East Side of Detroit who became world heavyweight champion. Joe (second from the right) got his start in the Golden Gloves competitions sponsored by the Detroit Free Press, and was a member of the 1934 team that fought in Chicago. He won the world heavyweight title from Jim Braddock in 1937. (Free Press)

JACK BLACKBURN, who is running with Louis in this training session for a bout with Bob Pastor in Detroit, is given a lot of credit for helping to make Joe the champ. With them, at right, is another handler, Larry Amandee. (Free Press)

[186]

ANYTIME JOE fought it was sure to bring out the cheering crowds, particularly when the extras hit the streets in what was then known as Detroit's "Black Bottom." (Free Press)

PONTIAC, celebrating its many years of progress in November 1936, held this parade on Saginaw (looking south here from Huron) as one of the highlights. Settlers from Detroit, following the Saginaw trail, picked the spot where it crossed the Clinton River to establish Pontiac in 1818. Swamps covering the land beyond Detroit made it difficult to get to, and some went there by way of Mount Clemens during the spring. It was a thriving community, however, by the time Michigan became a state. (Burton)

INDUSTRIAL UNIONISM came into its own in the 1930s primarily from major organizing drives all over Michigan. New Year's Eve of 1936, at the Fisher Body Plant No. 1 in Flint, was the start, and the last major drive for the automotive industry was in April 1941, when Ford signed its historic contract with the UAW. Hours after the first sit-down strike had started, Democrat Frank Murphy became governor. Although a court had ordered ejection of the strikers, Murphy sent the National Guard to keep the peace rather than to evacuate the plants. After an agreement was reached with General Motors on March 21, 1937, the tempo of organization speeded up throughout the state.

GOVERNOR MURPHY ponders over the latest
sit-down report. (Wayne)

NATIONAL GUARDSMEN come marching into
downtown Flint. (Wayne)

EVERYBODY BECAME INVOLVED in the strike, including the women and children. One gambit in the Flint strike was to set up a women's day, in which club-waving wives, girl friends, and picket-sign-carrying children gave vivid evidence of their support for the sit-downers. (Wayne)

THE HAPPY MOMENT finally came when Berdene (Bud) Simons, chairman of the Fisher Plant No. 1 strike committee, stood before the men with the *Detroit Free Press* extra in his hand, to read aloud the good news that the strike was ended.

DOWN IN MONROE, efforts to organize the Republic Steel Company resulted in the use of tear gas to break up one demonstration, but shortly thereafter another rally *(below)* was put together by the UAW to protest the earlier attack. Placards refer to the Battle of the Overpass which had happened only a few days before, and to the treatment of other organizers. (Wayne)

MICHIGAN (the entire world, for that matter) was given a hero to worship in the 1930s, via radio. His name was Lone Ranger and he rode Silver and had a sidekick named Tonto; and he kept talking about Kee-Mosah-Bee all because one of the show's writers needed an Indian word and remembered the name of a camp he had attended years before. Brace Beemer, the energetic man in the middle here, is running through a rehearsal for the show in the studios of WXYZ, where it all began. (Osgood)

BRACE BEEMER and Silver, as people must have visualized them. (Free Press)

TWO OF FOOTBALL'S greatest careers—one coaching and the other playing—touched each other at the University of Michigan in the 1930s. Fielding (Hurry up) Yost who had taught football brilliantly since the late 1800s and had won 202, lost 43, and tied 11 games in 28 seasons of active coaching, retired as athletic director just about when Tom Harmon hit the campus. Harmon was all-American in 1939 and 1940, scored 33 touchdowns in three seasons, and in 1940 won football's two most noted trophies—the Heisman and Maxwell. Harmon distinguished himself later as an Army pilot in World War II and as a sports broadcaster.

ON THIS 1938 DAY, Fielding H. Yost turned over the reins as athletic director at the University of Michigan to Herbert (Fritz) Crisler. (Free Press)

"OLD 98" on the move against Illinois in a 1940 game at U of M Stadium. (Free Press)

UNTIL THEY BUILT the Mackinac
Bridge, lines that sometimes were 20
miles long, particularly during hunting
season, were the rule for people traveling
from the Lower to the Upper Peninsula.
The five car ferries available could carry
a total of 460 vehicles at one time. Here
is the *City of Petoskey* loading at the
Mackinaw City dock, while down the line
in the boondocks hunters have time
to chat. (Bridge)

THIS DREAM CAR was designed by Harley Earl for General Motors in 1938. So far advanced then that it attracted unusual attention, many of its features have become standard on cars today, including disappearing headlights. Ironically, the convertible model has practically disappeared now. (GM)

MRS. FRANK FITZGERALD, left, and Mrs. Wilbur M. Brucker, right, whose husbands were governors, shared the spotlight at a GOP women's reception with Mrs. Harry S. Toy and Mrs. Paul A. Voorheis after the November 6, 1934, election.

[194]

NO STATE FAIR is complete without the governor helping to auction off the prize steer. In 1940, Gov. Frank Fitzgerald had a hand in peddling champion Repeat Domino at 75 cents per pound. Fitzgerald, a long-time Republican leader,was elected in 1938, but died in office and was succeeded by colorful, eighty-year-old Luren Dickinson, a Bible-quoting, thoroughly religious man. Dickinson gained attention when he returned from a national governors' conference blasting the "moral looseness" he had witnessed there, and giving thanks that attending "Michigan girls came home unsullied and unaware of how near they had been to the brink." Also his frugality was devastating. He once took off on a speaking tour of the South's Bible Belt while an important decision was pending. He sent back a postcard in which he said that legislators should do less talking and more praying. At the end, he casually added word of his decision. (Free Press)

GOV. LUREN DICKINSON, an all-out leader of the prohibitionists, speaks to Jackson blacks at a 1939 event marking the seventy-fifth anniversary of the signing of the Emancipation Proclamation; oblivious, of course, to the sign behind him promoting Kooler Keg Beer. Dickinson was almost eighty years old, serving his seventh term as lieutenant-governor (an office separately elected from the governor's), when he became governor upon the death of Gov. Frank Fitzgerald. (Free Press)

AMONG PICTURESQUE SIGHTS offered by the Water Wonderland are its lighthouses. The famous one *(left)* stands near Harbor Rock on Isle Royale; the other *(below)* at an unidentified spot. (Free Press-Ford)

FOR MICHIGAN'S CATHOLICS, a major personality proved to be Edward Mooney who was installed as archbishop of the Detroit Diocese in August 1938. He replaced Bishop Michael Gallagher who had been in Detroit from 1918 until his death early in 1937. Another happy moment was when Mooney was made a cardinal in 1945. Noted *Free Press* photographer Tony Spina caught the drama of the installation and the personality of the then-archbishop in his new vestments. (Free Press)

THE MICHIGAN LANDSCAPE was once covered with oil derricks, such as these in a field near Clare. Today, the derricks are gone, but now pumps, with black-tipped armatures giving the impression of pelicans, can be seen in Albion, and all the way up through the heart of the state. Michigan's first commercial well was brought in in Saginaw County in 1925. By 1939, the year of this photograph, production had peaked to 23.4 million barrels of crude, to say nothing of billions of cubic feet of natural gas. By the 1950s, 20,000 wells had been drilled, and 9,100 produced oil and 1,300 gas. The remaining 9,000-plus were dry, but it cost the producers $600,000,000 to dig them. (State)

A MODERNISTIC PAINTING? Well, not quite. The view is of the General Motors Proving Grounds at Milford which, first used in 1924, has grown to include 79 miles of test roads on 4,009 acres, with a fulltime employment of 1,700. Road surfaces common to the United States and most European countries are used for the 76,900 miles of test driving done each day. (GM)

ALONG LAKE MICHIGAN, great fruit-growing and processing efforts are made from Benton Harbor to Traverse City, with such cities as Paw Paw in between developing into a grape-growing and wine-producing center. This sixteen-acre Benton Harbor market attracts buyers from all over to bid on the produce from nearby farms and orchards. In the background is the House of David cold-storage plant which includes equipment for sorting, packing, and storing. (AAA)

[198]

IN THE NORTHWEST, Traverse City is the heart of the world's greatest cherry-growing area. Each year it promotes that fact with a festival, complete with queens and unusual sights *(facing page, top)* in a parade that draws thousands. (AAA)

THE CHERRY FESTIVAL
Queen and her court in 1934.
(AAA)

LOOK ABOUT YOU and see the beauty of an icebreaker cutting a path for a handful of ships through the Detroit River. In recent years, it has become common for Great Lakes shipping to operate on an almost year-round basis. (Dowling)

[200]

Towards a New Start

MOVING INTO THE FORTIES, Michigan's first challenge was to serve as the Arsenal for Democracy, with all of its energies focused very early on World War II. Michigan had 613,542 persons serve in the Armed Forces in addition to its contributions at the manufacturing level.

Inevitably, of course, the war period brought problems. Most notable were the tensions created by racial differences, and in 1943 a major riot rocked Detroit and Michigan.

The postwar period brought new strikes as labor and management readjusted to peacetime production, but by the end of the 1950s, after the Korean war, Michigan again was finding itself on the verge of a new expansion.

[201]

THIS TIME, during World War II, the famous "Red Arrow" or 32nd Division fought in the South Pacific and again won plaudits for its efforts. Gov. Murray Van Wagoner took time in June of 1941, to go to Camp Livingston in Louisiana to greet the officers and men of the 125th Infantry, 32nd Division. (Free Press)

FEW DOUBTS AROSE about getting into World War II, as the reaction of these men on the line at Ford Motor Company shows. They are producing the last car for civilian use in February 1943, after which they immediately began to build thousands of Jeeps. Civilian automobile assembly lines would not start again until 1945. (Sorenson)

MEANWHILE, BACK HOME, these Hamtramck Blue Star Mothers prepared packages to send to the boys overseas, and some well-known names popped up in the news. Lt. Comdr. Harry Kipke, former football coach for the University of Michigan, for one, was reported to be recruiting for the Navy. Below, he takes time out to swear in the late Charles Creedon, who spent most of his life planning trips as the Detroit Tigers' traveling secretary. (Free Press)

UP IN Iron Mountain, where a division of Ford was building gliders, Henry Ford II took time out to accept an award for the plant's outstanding performance. He had just become president of the company. (Ford)

IN THE SPARTA AREA, attention during World War II focused on the presence of German war prisoners who lived in a tent city east of town. Another large group was housed at Fort Custer, where the barracks lent a comfortable touch including a few pinups. (Free Press)

THE TOP BRASS of General Motors made an unusual appearance together on January 11, 1940, the day the twenty-five millionth General Motors car was produced. A scroll signed by seventy-five veteran assembly-line employes was presented to (left to right) M. E. Coyle, then general manager of Chevrolet; Harlow H. Curtice, then general manager of Buick and later GM president; Alfred P. Sloan, Jr., then GM chairman; C. S. Mott, vice president and director; C. E. Wilson, then executive vice president and later GM president; and William S. Knudsen, then GM president. (GM)

ANOTHER TIGER GREAT was about to bow out, so they held Charley Gehringer Day at Briggs Stadium, and Manager Del Baker (right) presented Charley with a desk set as a gift from his teammates. That year brought an additional reward since the Tigers won the pennant and then the World Series by beating the Chicago Cubs, 4 games to 3. (Free Press)

THE FAMOUS PRODUCTION LINE of hockey was so dubbed by Jack Adams, the general manager. Gordie Howe, Sid Abel, and Ted Lindsey (left to right) played their first full season together in 1947-48. In the next years the Red Wings finished second one time, and then won four league championships in a row and two Stanley Cups. Gordie Howe, amazingly, was still playing more than twenty-five years later. (DHM)

WHEN TELEVISION ARRIVED in Michigan in the late 1940s, a program that made a hit was the Schoolhouse, featuring Dick Osgood. It had been elaborately produced as a radio show, so the transition to the screen was a simple one. During a radio performance at the Capitol Theater on a Saturday morning, Osgood managed to get the Seven Dwarfs to make an appearance. They were in town promoting their famous Disney show.

AS THE 1940s ENDED, television had become part of life. The first stars were people like Edythe Fern Melrose, the Lady of Charm, who effectively used the medium to demonstrate her cooking and other tips to women. She also helped to show the mobility of TV by presenting her show from various spots in the Detroit area. (Osgood)

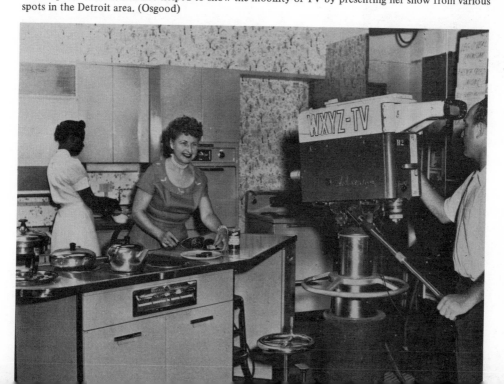

THEY STARTED IN TENTS and barns, but Michigan's straw hat theatres have today progressed to more sophisticated quarters. Just one phase of the wide variety of cultural activity in the state, the local theatres and musical groups on a for-fun basis involve thousands. (AAA)

[206]

A MISSISSIPPI STEAMBOAT? Well, not quite. This is the Suwanee Riverboat dock at Greenfield Village, one of America's most important historical centers. First put together by Henry Ford, the village contains a major collection of Americana, from the first automobiles to the courthouse in which Abraham Lincoln practiced law in Springfield, Illinois. This was the 1952 Old Country Fair, an event which has been expanded greatly over the years. (Greenfield)

EVERY MICHIGAN city saw its population boom during the war years, but none more so than Detroit, and with that boom came problems, particularly at the racial level. For some years, there had been a gradual build-up of tensions in Detroit, and by 1943 the situation became critical. Finally, there was an explosion. On a hot, humid Sunday—June 20, 1943—rumors flew through "Black Bottom," the black community that centered around Hastings Street, of attacks on blacks at Belle Isle. By nightfall fighting had broken out, and in the next few days, 34 people were killed, 23 of them blacks, 1,800 were treated for injuries, and property damage was in the millions.

THE INTENSITY OF feeling can be discerned as blacks are being chased by whites. This wild, rock-throwing scene was on one of Detroit's side streets, while out on Woodward Avenue, in the shadows of the downtown area, crowds milled about as cars were tipped over and burned.

MAYOR EDWARD JEFFRIES and Gov. Harry Kelly (in the straw hat) finally agreed they needed help, and a call went out for the U.S. troops. They came into Detroit and were bivouacked at Northwestern Field.

RACIAL HARMONY had its advocates, such as the Sojourner Truth Women's Group here. Eventually the city, and even later the state, established civil rights commissions, and Mrs. Geraldine Bledsoe, in black hat and coat, standing directly behind pulpit, emerged as one of Michigan's most-respected leaders in the battle for human rights. (Wayne)

UNTIL THE 1970s, when Gerald Ford finally made the grade, Michigan might well have been considered the leading home of would-be presidents in the country. Lewis Cass was nominated by the Democratic party in 1848 but lost because he felt that each state should have the right to determine for itself whether it would allow slavery or not. One hundred years later, another man from Michigan, Thomas Dewey, was running on the Republican ticket and lost to Harry Truman in what many consider the greatest upset in political history. Dewey had also run and lost in 1944. Dewey was born in Owosso, studied at U of M, then took his law degree at Columbia University, and stayed in New York to practice law. He became governor of New York in 1943, and served three terms.

OWOSSO, THE BIRTHPLACE of a candidate, called attention that one of its own was running for president. (Free Press)

ANOTHER MICHIGAN MAN, Sen. Arthur Vandenberg made a strong bid for the Republican presidential nomination in 1942, but it went to Wendell Wilkie, who lost to Franklin Roosevelt in the precedent-setting third try by FDR. Gov. Luren Dickinson and Edward Barnard, long a political power in Wayne County, stand directly under the banner here, just after Vandenberg's name was placed in nomination in Philadelphia. (Free Press)

[209]

DEMOCRATS GOT THEIR chance to push a presidential candidate in 1952, when Gov. G. Mennen "Soapy" Williams made a tentative bid at the Chicago convention. He didn't have a chance, however, for quite the opposite reason that defeated Lewis Cass. When Soapy led a fight to insure civil rights for all blacks in all states, some delegations threatened to walk out of the convention. (Free Press)

IDYLLIC WAS THE SETTING—and that's the way the wedding worked out, too. This was the wedding party when G. Mennen Williams and Nancy Quirk of Ypsilanti were married in June 1937. (Free Press)

ALWAYS EXTRA IMPORTANT is New Year's Day of every fourth year now, when a new governor is inaugurated. In 1941, when Murray Van Wagoner stepped into that office, he led the Grand March at the Masonic Temple in Lansing. The third man behind him, walking with a cane, is Harry Kelly, who was newly-elected secretary of state, and would become governor in 1943. Democrats were particularly happy to be dancing because they had been out of the executive mansion since Frank Murphy stepped down in 1938. (Free Press)

THE MOST COLORFUL of almost all Michigan governors was Kim Sigler, an impeccably-dressed former cowboy, one-time rancher, and amateur boxer who was elected in 1946 but decisively beaten by G. Mennen Williams in 1948. Sigler at nineteen had come to Michigan from Nebraska, got his law degree at University of Detroit, and gained public attention in 1943 as special prosecutor of a state grand jury investigation that brought the *Detroit Free Press* a Pulitzer Prize. His hobby, flying, led to his death in a crash in 1953. (Free Press)

THE YEAR'S HIGHLIGHT for many
fishermen is when the smelt run comes
to Michigan every spring. This time, in
April 1949, smelt-rushing was allowed
at 11 p.m., on little Cold Creek at
Beulah in Benzie County. In Washington
one year, Sen. Prentiss Brown, Smelt
Queen Barbara Banks of Escanaba,
Congressman Fred Bradley, and Senator
Vandenberg enjoyed a treat of Michigan
smelt in the congressional dining room.
(Free Press)

JAMES RIDDLE HOFFA was by the mid-1940s one of the most powerful men in the union movement, having established himself as undisputed leader of the Teamsters in Michigan and as a strong contender for national office. But in 1946, he faced a slight problem. He was charged by a grand jury with extortion because of alleged Teamster efforts to force independent grocers who were hauling their own meat and supplies from packing houses to pay into the Teamsters' treasury. The charge was reduced to violation of a state labor law, and he paid $500 in costs and agreed not to try to unionize the independent grocers. He's shown here with attorney George Fitzgerald (left) and Bert Brennan, another Teamsters official, at one of his many court hearings on the charges. By 1957, Hoffa was elected national Teamsters president and was being feted (below) with bigger-than-life decorations made of ice. Hoffa mysteriously disappeared in 1975 and is presumed dead. (Free Press)

FEW THINGS BRING a greater number of Michiganians together in one spot than Band Day at the University of Michigan Stadium each fall. Almost 150 high school bands perform. The first time, *(above)* on November 12, 1949, about fifty managed to work together to salute John Phillip Sousa, but in a couple of years they would cover the whole field and leave no room for maneuvering. (U. of M.) (U. of M.)

FROM ALL OVER the state they came to celebrate the tenth anniversary of the founding of the UAW-CIO with a big dinner at the Book's Cadillac Hotel in Detroit. Walter Reuther was sitting at the far left of the head table, and R. J. Thomas held center stage as president. It wasn't until a couple of years later that Reuther moved into the top spot. (Wayne)

PARKING METERS, power mowers, and women in saddle shoes. . . . It's the 1950s, and Bad Axe is beginning to show the signs of a new era. Bad Axe, sitting strategically near the tip of the Thumb area, is a commercial center and way station for thousands of vacationers who head for the beaches around Caseville and other spots. (Free Press)

IT SEEMS INCREDIBLE, but this was the scene at Boyne Mountain in 1948, when Everett Kircher started his first ski resort, with a second-hand ski lift. Twenty-five years later, the Boyne Mountain area had become one of America's outstanding resort centers. This effort helped trigger a multi-million dollar building boom in housing, and the state became a year-round vacation spot. Gov. Soapy Williams was among the resort's first visitors, although it appears he is more interested in photography than in schussing. (Boyne)

HOW TO TRANSFORM a lot of sand into a beach might well be the title of these pictures. In the late thirties, six southeastern counties got together and formed the Huron-Clinton Metropolitan Authority to build parks in the Huron River-Clinton River valley areas. One of its first efforts was a major beach outside of Mount Clemens on Lake St. Clair that took five years to finish at a cost of about 5 million dollars, and even then boasted an intricate sewer system to prevent pollution. (Free Press)

[217]

IT WAS AS IF IT HAPPENED in Detroit when the *Noronic,* queen of the Great Lakes fleet, burned at dockside in Toronto on the morning of September 17, 1949. She had stopped in Detroit and then gone on to pick up another large group of excursionists in Cleveland, before heading for Toronto. The tragedy stunned Michigan, for there were many from the state among the 119 who were killed.

AS FLAMES SWEPT the luxury vessel, passengers rushed to starboard, helping to tip the doomed ship.

A CLOSEUP VIEW of the holocaust, with firemen searching for bodies. (Free Press)

AN HISTORIC MOMENT came when Walter Reuther (left) signed a five-year contract with General Motors in 1950, guaranteeing one of the country's most extended periods of labor peace. Exuberant besides Reuther were (left to right) T. Arthur Johnstone, the UAW director of the GM department; Harry W. Anderson, then GM vice president in charge of personnel staff; and Louis G. Seaton, then director of GM labor relations. (GM)

THE 50 MILLIONTH General Motors car had been produced by 1954, and that called for a celebration—in Flint, where GM was born. More than 100,000 people saw the parade of GM's Golden Carnival. (Free Press)

THEN MICHIGAN BECAME ONE. When the Mackinac Bridge was opened for the first time to traffic in November 1957, it was one of those dreams that came true, thanks to the genius of designer David B. Steinmann and an expenditure of about $90,000,000. Its 26,444-foot length permits the biggest of lake ships to pass under its center span, which is 148 feet above the waterline; but its physical dimensions are only secondary to what the bridge has meant in unifying a state. And, in a real sense, it's also an important tie between two nations. This picture was taken by the *Detroit Free Press'* Tony Spina, who has the great knack of being able to dramatize even the most static situation.

BRIDGES OF PEACE *(facing page)* are the kind that Michigan has built in the years since the first Frenchmen came to explore the wilderness for a pathway to the Far East or to profit from the furs of animals. Where else are there three that tie one country to another like the Ambassador Bridge at Detroit, the Blue Water Bridge at Port Huron, and the International Bridge at Sault Ste. Marie? Michigan, surrounded by water by nature, has succeeded in reaching out to its fellow men by means of steel and concrete, opening the way to better understanding. It augurs well for its future and that of the millions who make it their home. (AAA-Free Press)

STARTING FROM THE NORTH, one can sweep under the International Bridge *(right)* that joins together the two Sault Ste. Maries and then head through the locks.

TRAVEL SOUTH and under the Blue Water Bridge (shown below under construction) which joins Port Huron and Sarnia; and wind up . . . sailing under the Ambassador Bridge *(bottom)*, and down into Lake Erie.

LOOK ABOUT YOU and see the incomparable Traverse Bay area in this masterpiece of clouds, water, and land taken by Tony Spina. You're looking west, with a piece of Torch Lake at the bottom of the picture and the Leelanau Peninsula looming large beyond Mission Point and the West Bay. (Free Press)

Index

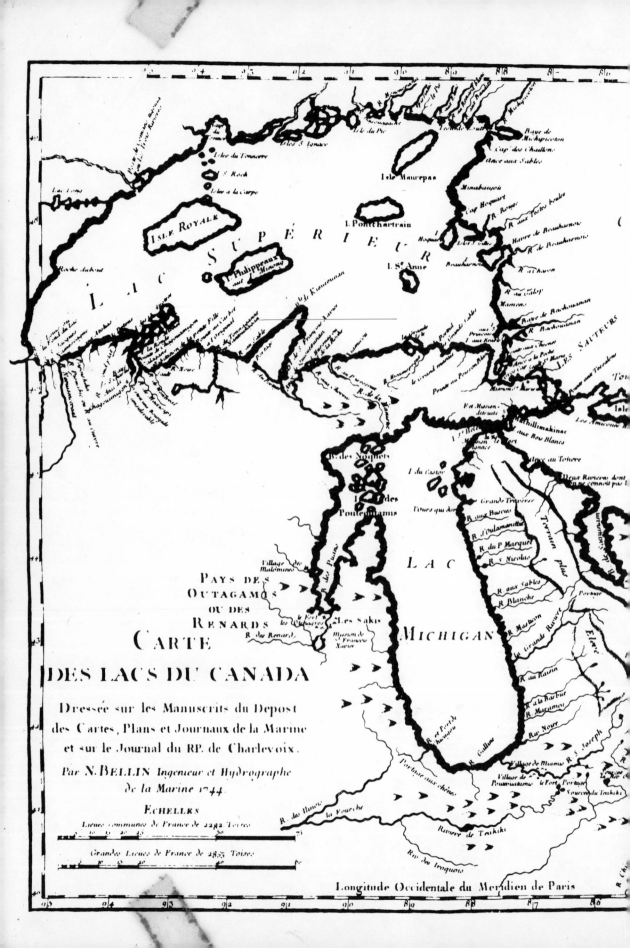

CARTE

DES LACS DU CANADA

Dressée sur les Manuscrits du Depost
des Cartes, Plans et Journaux de la Marine
et sur le Journal du RP. de Charlevoix.

Par N. BELLIN Ingenieur et Hydrographe
de la Marine 1744.

ECHELLES

Lieues communes de France de 2282 Toises

Grandes Lieues de France de 2853 Toises

Longitude Occidentale du Meridien de Paris